36 One-day
Discovery Tours
Fun Places to Drive Within and From
Minneapolis and St. Paul
BY Carvel Lee
ILLUSTRATIONS BY THE AUTHOR
NODIN PRESS

Copyright 1990 by Carvel Lee
All rights reserved. No part of this book may be reproduced in any form without the permission of Nodin Press, except for review purposes.

ISBN 0-931714-75-3

Library of Congress Catalogue Card No.

Nodin Press, a division of Micawber's, Inc.
525 North Third Street
Minneapolis, MN 55401

Revised and Expanded Edition, 1997

W N S E

CL

INTRODUCTION

Travel is a popular pastime today. Swift jet planes shrink the globe and make distant destinations common. Has flying to faraway places made us ignore exciting possibilities at home?
How well do you know our nearby cities or the at-our-door-step area? Have you been to Elysian or Wasioja? They are practically our neighbors. You won't find a higher quality of life or richer history, traditions and culture anywhere than we have right in our backyard. We have pioneer and Indian trails, folk legends and ethnic diversity. Local museums have diligently preserved past records and artifacts for our present enjoyment and enlightenment. You will encounter places of beauty and interest in both urban and rural settings. There are a wealth of fine eating places and pristine picnic sites.

These outings appeal to tour groups, seniors, families, school field trips, businesses and churches. Visitors or new residents will quickly get acquainted with the special all-season allure of our area.

ABOUT THE AUTHOR

For twelve years Carvel Lee has innovated and completed one-a-month trips, no two alike, that radiate from the Twin Cities. Tour members' enthusiasm for these tours necessitated one to three coaches for each outing. She has explored extensively with her family which includes two children. These lively, homey outings are the culmination of her exuberant zest for discovery.

Carvel Lee is the author/illustrator of over one hundred books and is a community leader in numerous areas. Her sincere wish is that *ONE-DAY DISCOVERY TOURS* will be your personal guide to exciting adventure with miles of smiles bringing joy to you. Have a happy day!

"I've driven this way many times, but I never knew that these places existed," is a typical comment from tour members. To experience any area fully you have to slow down, stop and really look. It's not how much distance you can cover, but how much you can discover.

Take time to stop and listen to the crickets chirp and watch the geese overhead winging in formation. Be curious and observant, ask questions and find that most townspeople are delighted with your interest. An early start will mean that you can browse leisurely at interest points.

Go with an open mind. Follow your own unhurried getaway schedule. Make it a day of pleasure and relaxation.

Choose from fifteen thousand lakes, parks, marinas and state trails for biking, hiking, and snowmobile and horseback riding. We have zoos, museums, waterfalls, sparkling rivers and creeks, theaters, skyscrapers and log cabins, deluxe shopping and specialty stores. It's a whole world of discovery. The advance work has been done for you—set yourself free!

CONTENTS

TOUR NO.	TITLE AND DESTINATION	PAGE
	INTRODUCTION	
	CONTENTS	
	TOUR SUGGESTIONS	5
1	BUNNY HOP SCENIC SIGHTSEEING TOUR Chanhassen, Shakopee, Savage and Prior Lake	6-7
2	MISSISSIPPI RIVER RAMBLE St. Anthony, Islands of Peace, Nicollet Island and the *Anson Northrup*	8-9
3	SWEDISH DALA HORSE COUNTRY OUTING Mora and Anoka, Isanti and Kanabec Counties	10-11
4	HEART OF ST. PAUL Downtown St. Paul Walking Tour	12-13
5	ST. PAUL PERIMETER SWING Bandana Square, Gibbs Farm, and a Scenic Lake	14-15
6	A SAILOR DARES TO DREAM White Bear Lake	16-17
7	BUTTERFLY BYWAYS Cannon Falls, Zumbrota, Red Wing, Durand	18-19
8	HARBOR COVES AND A CRYSTAL CAVE Afton, Hudson, Spring Valley, and Menomonie	20-21
9	METRO MINNEAPOLIS Downtown Minneapolis Walking Tour	22-23
10	DISCOVER THE UNUSUAL Do you know these Twin Cities places?	24-25
11	MAJESTIC MINNETONKA Excelsior, Spring Park, Mound, Orono and Wayzata	26-27
12	SUBURBAN SECRETS Burnsville, Eagan, Rosemount, Apple Valley, Farmington, Lakeville and Empire	28-29
13	MANSIONS AND STEAMBOATS Hastings, Prescott and Cottage Grove	30-31
14	KARL OSKAR AND SWEDISH SETTLERS Forest Lake, Chisago City, Lindstrom, Center City, Taylors Falls and Scandia	32-33
15	MINNEAPOLIS ARTS AND ANTIQUES Variety of Artistic Experiences	34-35
16	FOUR FAMOUS PERSONS TREK St. Cloud, Little Falls and Sauk Centre	36-37
17	HAPPY HOOTENANNY Belle Plaine, St. Peter and Mankato	38-39
18	MINNEAPOLIS, CITY OF LAKES Chain of Lakes, Powderhorn, Diamond and Loring Lakes	40-41
19	A TRAGIC FIRE AND LAKELAND LORE Hinckley, Mille Lacs Lake and Brainerd	42-43
20	COUNTRYSIDE AND LITTLE MOUNTAIN Monticello, Big Lake and Elk River	44-45
21	VALLEY VENTURE FOR ENTERTAINMENT Minnesota Valley's Attractions Beckon	46-47
22	CITY AND COUNTRY PLEASURES Rochester and Lovely Bluff Area Towns	48-49
23	ANNANDALE ADVENTURE Buffalo, Cokato, Annandale and Waverly	50-51
24	BANDITS AND BLANKETS Faribault and Northfield, History and Tradition	52-53
25	PARKLAND AND A GOLD STRIP Do you know Bloomington and Richfield?	54-55
26	GERMAN HERITAGE New Ulm, Willkommen to Gemutlichkeit	56-57
27	DRUMS AND THE SONG OF HIAWATHA Minnehaha Falls, Fort Snelling and Mendota	58-59
28	LUMBERJACKS AND GANGSTERS St. Croix Falls, Hayward and the Hideout	60-61
29	WHERE ARE ELYSIAN AND SAKATAH? Waterville, Elysian, Madison Lake and New Prague	62-63
30	SCENIC ROADS AND FLYING CLOUDS Do you know Edina and Eden Prairie?	64-65
31	TWO TOWERING RIVER BLUFFS Two river cities, Winona and La Crosse	66-67
32	BOARDWALKS AND MEMORIES Mantorville, Albert Lea, Owatonna and Austin	68-69
33	PIPESTONE AND PEACEPIPES Pipestone National Monument Tour	70-71
34	THE BIRTHPLACE OF MINNESOTA Stillwater, Somerset and Willow River State Park	72-73
35	CHILDREN ON TOURS	74
36	DISCOVER AND EXPLORE LOCAL ATTRACTIONS	75
	ARE YOU A VISITOR? HERE ARE HELPFUL IDEAS TO MAKE EXPLORING MINNESOTA EASY EXPLORE MINNESOTA SHOP	76
	MALL OF AMERICA, KNOTT'S CAMP SNOOPY TWO HISTORIC AND SCENIC TROLLEY RIDES	77
	DO YOU KNOW MINNESOTA?	78
	RESOURCES TO HELP YOU TRAVEL	79
	HAPPY MEMORIES	80

MAP SYMBOLS

These symbols are used throughout the book. Each map will have symbols to represent such things as interest points, mileage and stops. Take time to discover what is to be found at these locations and add enjoyment to your tour.

HIGHWAYS

US **INTERSTATE** **STATE** **COUNTY**

 **INTEREST POINT**

 **FOOD**

 **HISTORIC SITE**

 **ANTIQUES**

 **PARK**

 **SCENIC ROUTE**

 **MUSEUM**

DIRECTION SYMBOLS

These compass symbols show the general direction of the tour routes.

MAPS ARE NOT TO SCALE

TOUR SUGGESTIONS

WHETHER YOU ARE A MINNESOTA RESIDENT OR A VISITOR, RELAX, RAMBLE AND REALLY LOOK AND SEE.

1. TAKE YOUR TIME! THAT'S IMPORTANT! Rushing is fine if all you want to see is freeways and billboards whizzing past in a blur. Why not slow down and explore? Don't just drive by—drive in. That's what this guidebook is all about. SLOW DOWN and SEE.
2. TAKE A MAP. Use this aid to further your exploring. The State of Minnesota has many maps and brochures available.
3. PLAN YOUR DAY. Talk it over and decide which tour fits your mood, the season and your interests on this particular day. Is it a weekend? Some business or group tours may not be available. Want to picnic or eat out? Look for a restaurant or park at a half-way point.
4. MAKE RESERVATIONS where needed to smooth your trip.
5. START EARLY. If you begin your day late, you will have to skip stops. Give yourself a full day's fun.

BUS GROUPS AND FIELD TRIPS

1. Advance planning is essential for large groups. Notify museums, restaurants and coffee stops so they will be prepared with extra food, additional guides or help to serve your group.
2. Park route permits are required for buses in Minneapolis. Call the Minneapolis Park and Recreation Board, 612/348-2226.
3. Have a time schedule, allowing sufficient exit or loading time at stops so your tour will meet return deadlines. Give a time limit to passengers before they leave the bus at each stop.
4. Take a head-count before you move on from each stop.

TOUR 1 BUNNY HOP SCENIC SIGHTSEEING TOUR

MINNESOTA
LANDSCAPE ARBORETUM

This tour, southwest of Minneapolis, is educational and interesting. It includes the shops at Chanhassen Dinner Theatres, a tour of the Minnesota Landscape Arboretum, a scenic Lake Minnewashta drive, viewing the old and new facilities at the Minnesota Women's Correctional Institute, a stop at the Shakopee Mdewakanton Sioux Community and browsing at the Burnsville Center.

There is a wide choice of restaurants in this tour area. You might wish to make reservations in advance or choose a picnic site.

INTEREST POINTS

1. CHANHASSEN Shops in CHANHASSEN DINNER THEATRES COMPLEX. Make reservations if you want the dinner-theatre, 612/934-1525.
2. MINNESOTA LANDSCAPE ARBORETUM 3675 Arboretum Drive. Guided tours available and tram-car rides through 3 miles of 5,000 types of perennials, annuals, herbs, shrubs and trees. You may picnic at the shelters or lunch in the cafeteria. Open year-round; call for information about hours, tours, plants in bloom, events, 612/443-2460. Modest fee, seniors free 2nd and 4th Fridays.
3. Scenic loop tour of LAKE MINNEWASHTA. See detail map.
4. In Shakopee, take Apgar to 6th, turn right 3 blocks to see the old and new MINNESOTA WOMEN'S CORRECTIONAL INSTITUTE.
5. Several restaurants are at Co. Rd. 17 (Spring Lake Rd.) and US 169. DANGERFIELD'S has windows that overlook a pond with waterfowl.
6. Head S off US 169 on MN 17 on a scenic country route to Co. Rd. 42. At Co. Rd. 83 turn S to drive through the SHAKOPEE MDEWAKANTON SIOUX COMMUNITY. Note the large buildings where Bingo is played and the giant tepee. Mystic Lake Casino is also here.
7. At Co. Rd. 42 and I-35W is the BURNSVILLE CENTER comprised of many shops on several levels all of which are enclosed.

8- Turn back on Co. Rd. 42 to MN 13 and go N to where
9. Co. Rd. 13 joins MN 101. Just W of this junction at Boone Ave. you will find the ANCHOR IRON CO. SHOP that specializes in handmade cast-iron items and a COUNTRY GALLERY, 612/445-3030. Just W adjacent on MN 101 are two TAXIDERMY SHOPS. Go W on MN 101 to US 169 and US 212 which will return you to US I-494.

RESTAURANTS ADJACENT TO ROUTE

A. Dangerfield's, 1583 E. 1st. St., 612/445-2245.
There are many other restaurants at this location near Co. Rd. 17 and US 169.

B. Minnesota Landscape Arboretum, Tea Room Cafeteria, MN 5 and MN 41, 612/443-2460.

C. Burnsville Center, a variety of snack and fast food shops in the mall, plus many fine restaurants at the junction of I-35W and Co. Rd. 42.

TOUR 1

CHANHASSEN, SHAKOPEE, SAVAGE, and PRIOR LAKE

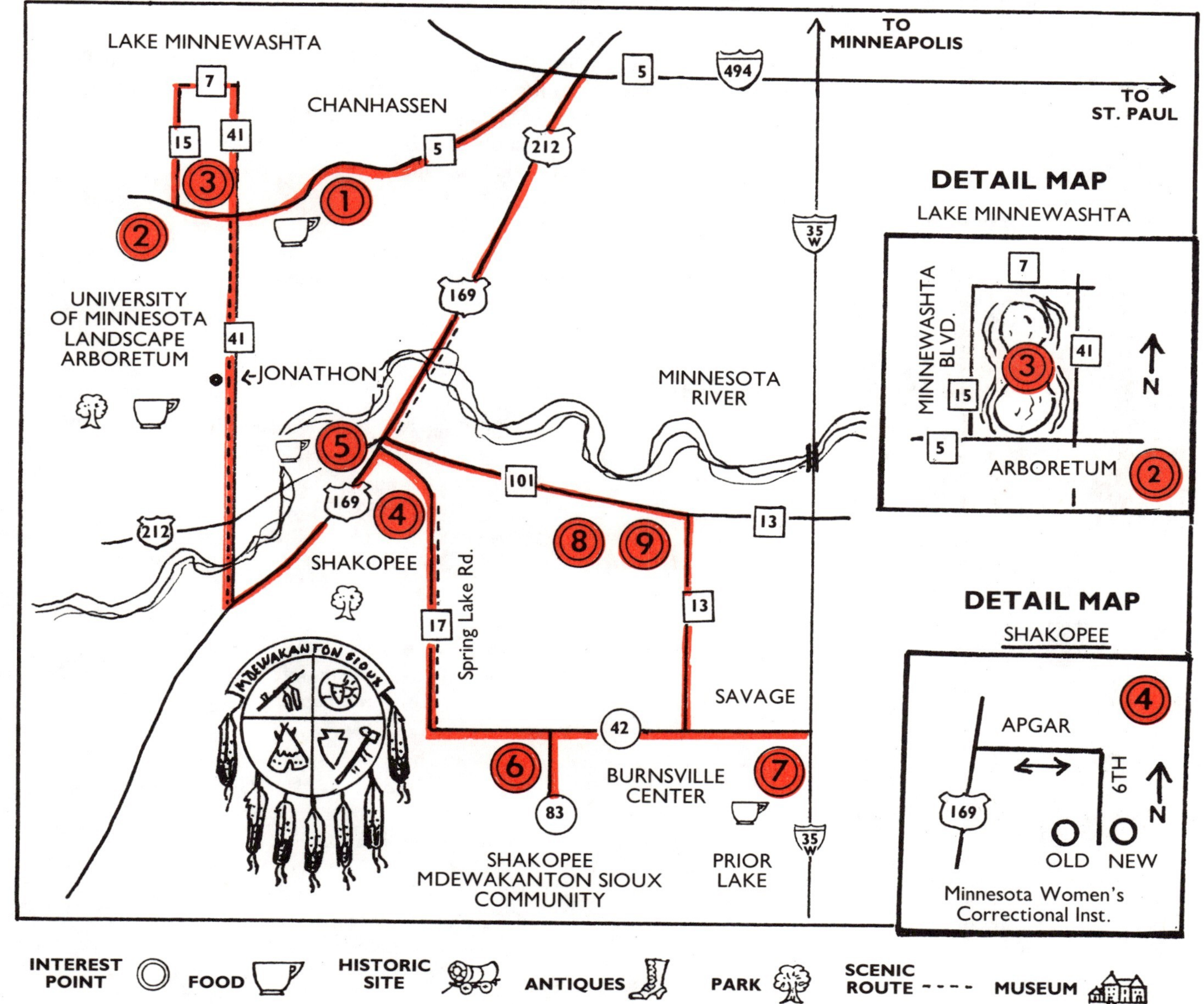

APPROX. TOTAL TOUR MILES 54

INTEREST POINT · FOOD · HISTORIC SITE · ANTIQUES · PARK · SCENIC ROUTE - - - - · MUSEUM

TOUR 2 MISSISSIPPI RIVER RAMBLE

JAMES FORD BELL
MUSEUM OF
NATURAL HISTORY

How well do you know the old grain mill area? This location is steeped in history. The first homes in Minneapolis were built in the St. Anthony vicinity about 1847. *Minni* is Dakota for water and *Apolis* is Greek for city. Flour mills and saw mills brought rapid growth, and Minneapolis became known as the "Flour Capitol" of the world.

A beautiful new Great River Road has picnic sites, shelters, biking and walking paths. This scenic route will eventually extend from Lake Itasca to the Gulf of Mexico. The *Anson Northrup*, a 400-passenger riverboat, makes excursions from the Boom Island Park dock.

INTEREST POINTS

1. ST. ANTHONY UPPER LOCK and DAM#1 1 Portland Ave. Turn N off Washington Ave., drive down under the Old Stone Bridge. Follow signs to the observation deck for city, dam and river views. Call 612/333-5336 for hours, no fee. Return up hill to the Great River Road. Note the WHITNEY HOTEL'S GARDEN AND FOUNTAINS.
2. Follow the GREAT RIVER ROAD and on the higher level to the left you will see the Fuji-Ya Restaurant, the MINNEAPOLIS POST OFFICE and the STAR TRIBUNE. On the right NICOLLET ISLAND can be seen across the river.
3. At Broadway turn right across the bridge. The old GRAIN BELT BREWERY is at Marshall St. Turn left at Marshall (which will become the East River Rd. further on) and you will pass the NORTHERN STATES POWER CO., the MINNEAPOLIS WATER WORKS, FMC CORPORATION and the ANOKA COUNTY RIVERFRONT REGIONAL PARK. The LOCKE HOUSE, an authentically preserved 1880 landmark, is at 6666 E. River Rd. Tours, call 612/421-0624.
4. ISLANDS OF PEACE, 200 Charles St., N.E., Fridley, is an unusual park with paths and bridges in a pristine setting that is handicap accessible. Call 612/757-3920 for information.
5. Exit right at Mississippi St. to the HOLLY CENTER where there is food and shopping. Turn right on University Ave. and continue until you reach 8th Ave. N.E.
6. Turn right at 8th Ave. N.E., and turn left into the BOOM ISLAND PARK. The *Anson Northrup* is docked here. Call 612/348-2226/227-1100 for excursion information.
7. NICOLLET ISLAND Return to University Ave. and turn right on 1st Ave. which will take you to Hennepin Ave. As you are approaching the Hennepin Ave. bridge turn right at W. Island Ave. to Nicollet Island. Circle the island and exit at Merriam to return to University Ave.
8. RIVERPLACE and ST. ANTHONY MAIN Exit at Bank St. to Riverplace at 25 Main St. S.E. and St. Anthony Main at 201 Main St. S.E. Explore the restaurants and unique shops. Take the River City Trolley 612/204-0000.
9. Return to University, driving through a portion of the UNIVERSITY OF MINNESOTA CAMPUS to Church St. (17th Ave.) for a tour of the JAMES FORD BELL MUSEUM OF NATURAL HISTORY, 10 Church St., 612/624-1852, fee. Cross University Ave. to 4th St. S.E., turn left to 35W which will take you to the Washington Ave. exit and return you to the tour starting point.

RESTAURANTS ADJACENT TO ROUTE

A. Old Country Buffet, 6540 University Ave., N.E., Fridley, 612/572-8627.

B. Nicollet Island Inn, 95 Merriam St., 612/331-1800/331-3035.

C Pracna on Main/Herman's 1890, 117 S.E. Main St., 612/379-2300.

TOUR 2

ST. ANTHONY AREA, ISLANDS OF PEACE, NICOLLET ISLAND, "ANSON NORTHRUP"

DETAIL MAPS

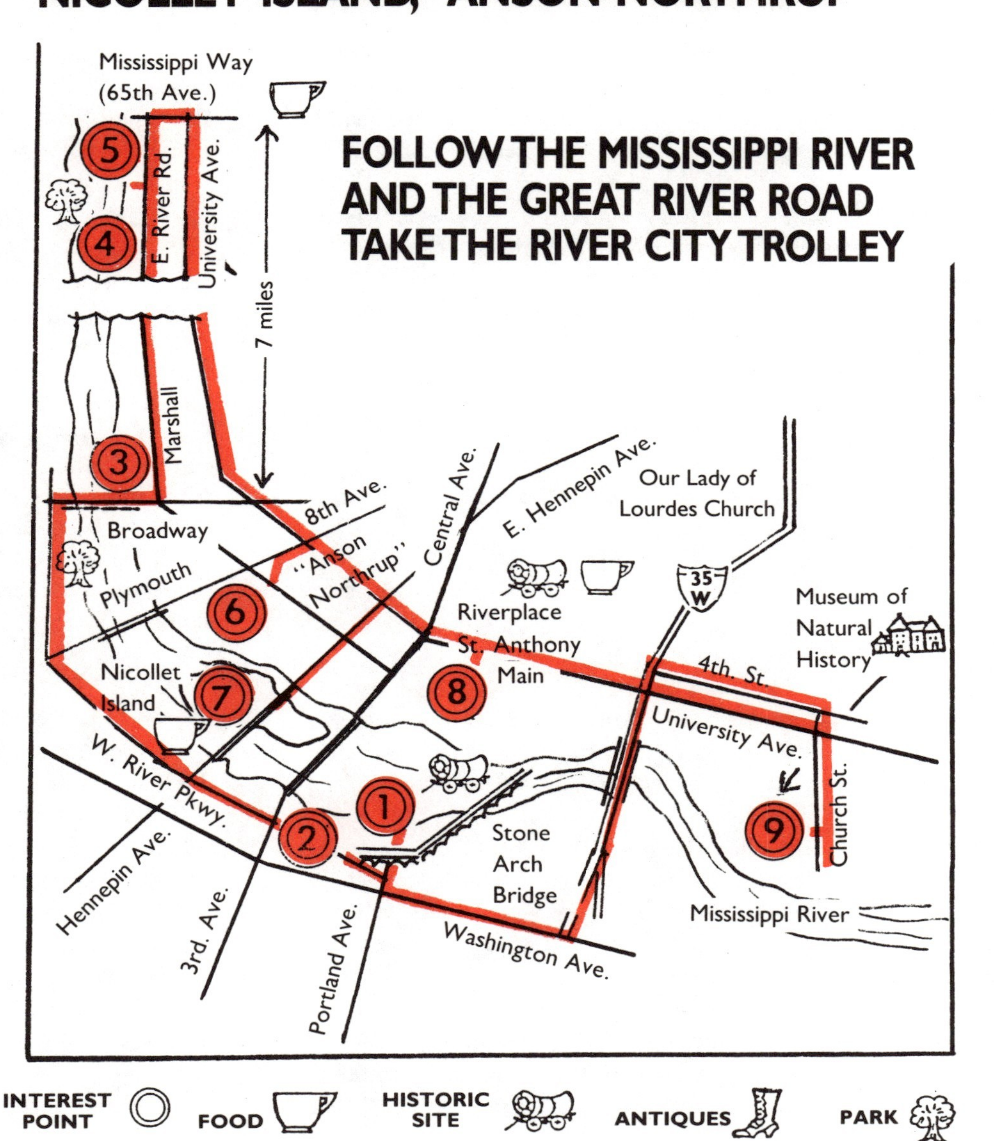

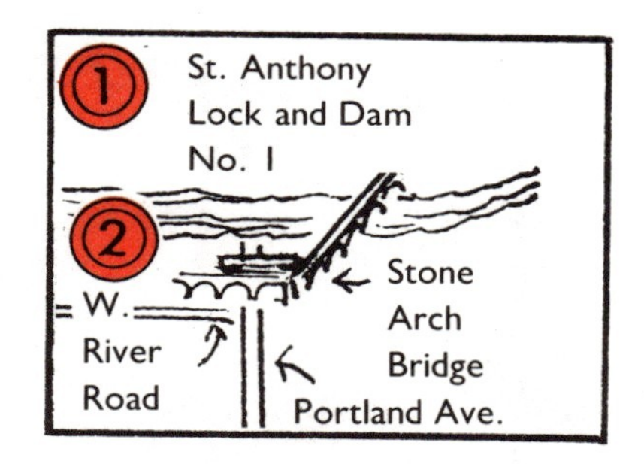

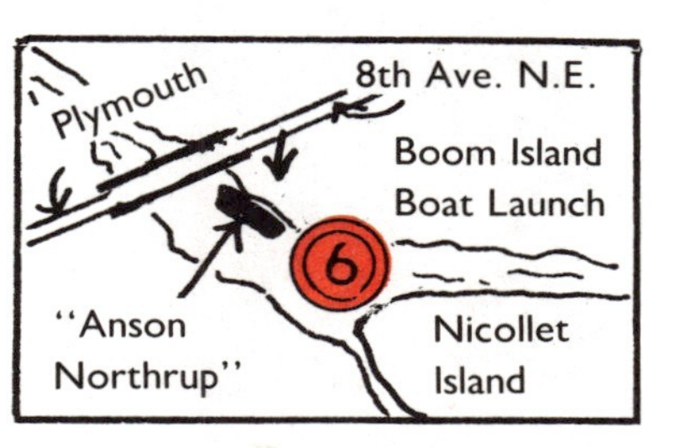

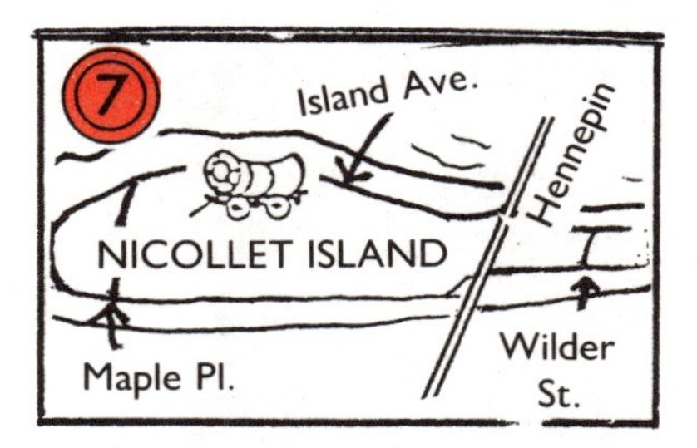

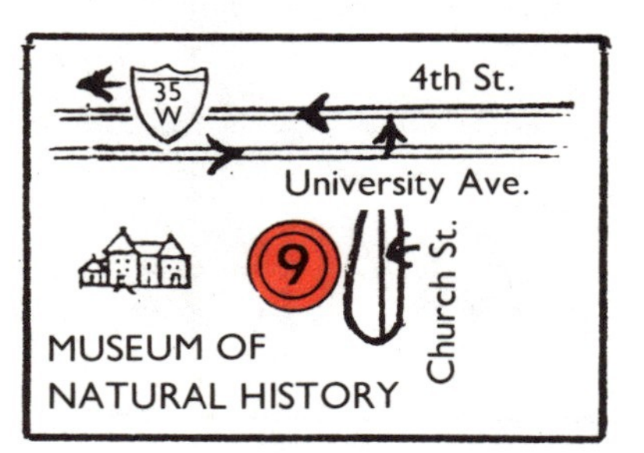

APPROX. TOTAL TOUR MILES 25 | INTEREST POINT | FOOD | HISTORIC SITE | ANTIQUES | PARK | SCENIC ROUTE - - - - | MUSEUM

TOUR 3 SWEDISH *DALA HORSE* COUNTRY OUTING

Relax with a day's ramble to Anoka County. Roll through small towns and farmland. Peat deposits underlie sandy soil. Marshes are rimmed with poplar, tamarack and oak. The Mississippi and Rum rivers plus many lakes make appealing scenery.

Several Indian tribes lived in Anoka territory. Father Hennepin, Joseph Belanger and Daniel Stanchfield were important in early history. Logs were floated down the rivers to St. Anthony sawmills. Anoka hoped to be a major metropolis, but populations centered in the Twin Cities area instead.

Much Kanabec County history is available for browsing at the Kanabec County Museum.

INTEREST POINTS

1. At MN 65 and Co. Rd. 242 turn W and go 2 mi. to the BUNKER HILLS REGIONAL PARK and the ANOKA COUNTY ACTIVITIES CENTER. There is a varied choice of recreation here: a greenhouse, picnic area, trails, horseback riding, hiking, golf, archery and playground (see detail map).
2. Return to MN 65 and go N to Bunker Lake Blvd. (or Co. Rd. 116), turn left and go 3 mi. to 3331 Bunker Lake Blvd. to the ROUND BARN. You will find handcrafted items, antiques and collectables. Open Tues.-Sat., 612/427-5321.

   Return to MN 65 and go N to CAMBRIDGE, named after Cambridge, Massachusetts from where the town's first settlers came. Yet even here there is a Swedish Festival each year in June with a parade and a rope-pulling contest across the river.
3. At MORA turn W to Main St. and then turn left to view the 25-foot DALA HORSE (DALECARLIAN) considered a holy animal in ancient Sweden. Mora's quaint shops sell replicas. Mora is SISTER CITY to Mora, Sweden. Dala Days are in mid-June and the international Vasa Loppet Cross Country Ski Race is held here in February. Dine at the De Dutch Huis for good food and ethnic atmosphere.
4. Follow the detail map to the KANABEC COUNTY MUSEUM, modest fee, 10 a.m. to 4:30 p.m., Mon.-Sat., 320/679-1665.
5. From Mora turn W on Co. Rd. 23 and turn S on Co Rd. 47 drive through open countryside and rural towns to ANOKA. Here you will find history, river parks and food. "Halloween Capital of the World." this well-deserved title sets the mood for the OCTOBER PUMPKIN BOWL held each year. The Anoka Chamber of Commerce phone number is 612/421-7130. The RUM RIVER and DAM are scenic attractions. The ANOKA COUNTY HISTORICAL MUSEUM is at 1900 Third Ave. S., 612/421-0600. A 17-room home, 1904 COLONIAL HALL contains local history and resource library, Tues.-Fri., 12:30-4 p.m. by reservation.

RESTAURANTS ADJACENT TO ROUTE

A. Majestic Oaks Restaurant, MN 65 and Bunker Lake Blvd., 612/755-2140

B. MORA, De Dutch Huis Restaurant, 17 N. Main, 320/679-1761, restaurant and bakery, open 7 days a week.

C. ANOKA, Back Street Pizza, historic building, 213 Jackson St., 612/421-7522.

Greenhaven Restaurant, 2800 Greenhaven Rd., 612/427-8660.

Oakwood Inn, 710 E. River Rd., 612/427-8295.
Perkins, 601 W. Main St., 612/421-0160.
Embers, 1500 S. Ferry St., 612/421-6350.

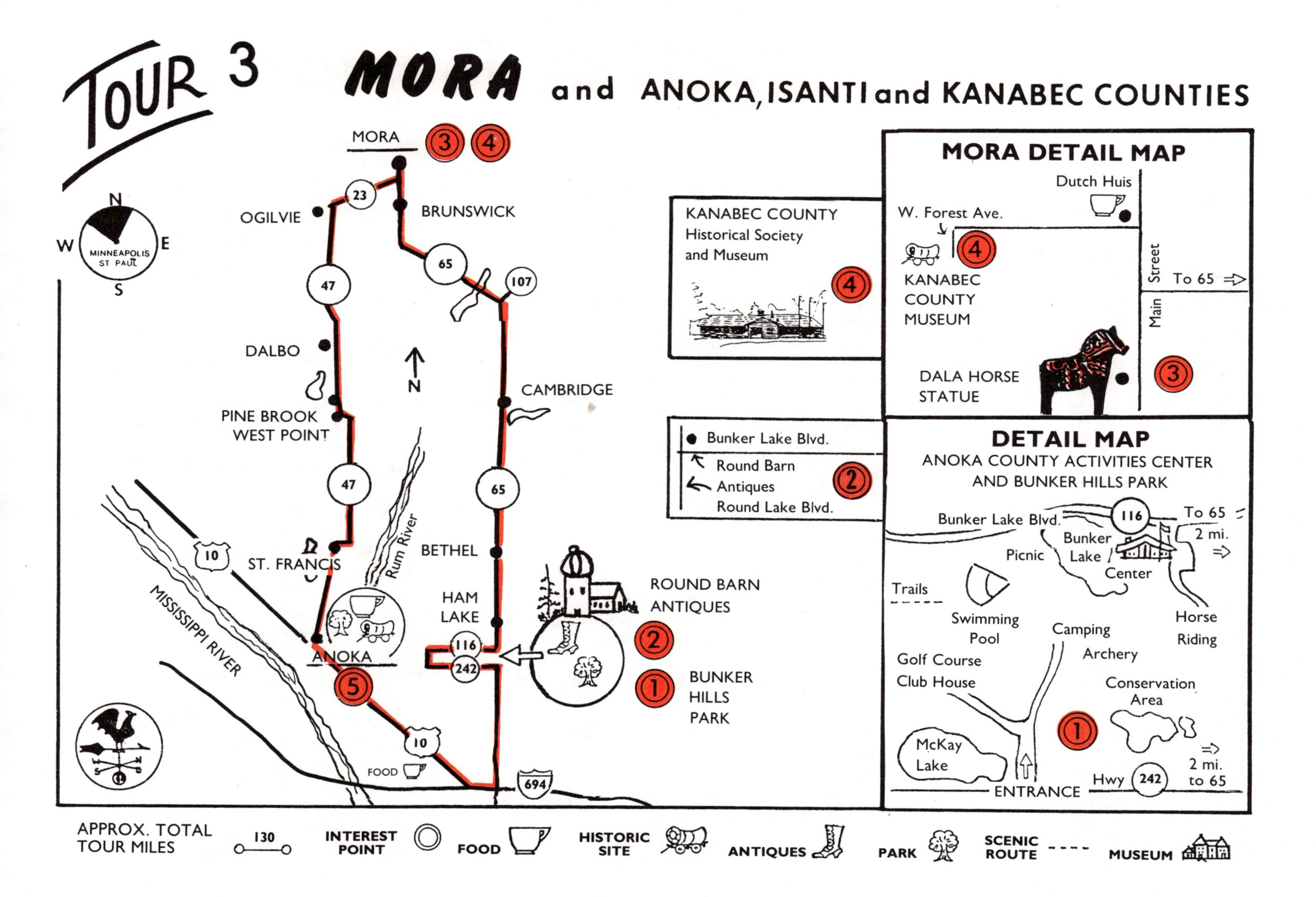

TOUR 3
MORA and ANOKA, ISANTI and KANABEC COUNTIES
MORA
OGILVIE
BRUNSWICK
DALBO
PINE BROOK
WEST POINT
CAMBRIDGE
ST. FRANCIS
Rum River
BETHEL
HAM LAKE
ANOKA
MISSISSIPPI RIVER
ROUND BARN ANTIQUES
BUNKER HILLS PARK
FOOD
N
W
E
S
MINNEAPOLIS ST PAUL
KANABEC COUNTY Historical Society and Museum
Bunker Lake Blvd.
Round Barn Antiques
Round Lake Blvd.
MORA DETAIL MAP
Dutch Huis
W. Forest Ave.
KANABEC COUNTY MUSEUM
DALA HORSE STATUE
Main Street
To 65
DETAIL MAP
ANOKA COUNTY ACTIVITIES CENTER AND BUNKER HILLS PARK
Bunker Lake Blvd.
To 65 2 mi.
Bunker Lake
Picnic
Center
Trails
Swimming Pool
Camping
Horse Riding
Archery
Golf Course Club House
Conservation Area
McKay Lake
ENTRANCE
Hwy 242
2 mi. to 65
APPROX. TOTAL TOUR MILES 130
INTEREST POINT
FOOD
HISTORIC SITE
ANTIQUES
PARK
SCENIC ROUTE
MUSEUM

TOUR 4

HEART OF ST. PAUL

In 1841, Father Lucian Galtier built a church called the Chapel of St. Paul, the name later given to the city that developed on this site. James J. Hill was a railroad baron when eleven railroads served the area. St. Paul cherishes its vintage buildings and is proud of its heritage.

NATIVE AMERICAN
GOD OF PEACE

INTEREST POINTS

1. MINNNESOTA STATE CAPITOL Aurora at Cedar, 296-2881. This beautiful building has the largest unsupported marble dome in the world. More than 25 varieties of marble, limestone, sandstone and granite were used in the construction. Above the south entrance is a group of golden sculptured horses. The cornerstone was laid in 1898. Tours.
2. GALTIER PLAZA 366 Jackson St., 297-6738. A combination of fine stores, restaurants and cinemas.
3. MEARS PARK PLAZA Fourth St. at Sibley St. Adjacent to Lowertown where shops, restaurants, offices and housing give new life to a warehouse district, including an art gallery and theater.
4. FEDERAL COURTS BUILDING 316 N. Robert St., 222-5658.
5. CITY HALL and RAMSEY COUNTY COURTHOUSE Fourth St. at Wabasha St., 298-4012. This building houses city and county offices and boasts the famous Peace Memorial Statue by Carl Milles that represents "The Dream of Peace." Each of 18 floors is finished in a different wood from around the world. Tours.
6. RADISSON ST. PAUL HOTEL 11 E. Kellogg Blvd., 222-7711. Rotating Le Carrousel restaurant and glass elevators with river view.
7. MINNESOTA MUSEUM OF ART 305 St. Peter St., 224-7431. Self-guided tours.
8. PUBLIC LIBRARY and HILL REFERENCE LIBRARY 90 West Fourth St., 292-6206. Classic Italian Renaissance design. Guided tours. See the Minnesota Vietnam Memorial and the Children's Museum.
9. CIVIC CENTER Kellogg Blvd. at West Seventh St., 224-7361. Sports and entertainment events, arena, auditorium and theater.
10. ORDWAY MUSIC THEATRE 345 Washington St., 224-4222. A premiere performing arts center of music, theatre and dance.
11. LANDMARK CENTER 75 W. Fifth St., 292-3233. Performing and visual arts and civic activities in a restored 1894 building. Tours.
12. RICE PARK Fourth St. at Washington. Lively at all seasons with various activities.
13. CARRIAGE HILL PLAZA 14 W. Fifth St., 224-2865. Cobblestone corridors with specialty shops.
14. TOWN SQUARE, Seventh and Cedar Sts., 291-8900, 227-3307. Shops, restaurants and an enclosed park with waterfalls and garden areas. Skyways lead to 19th-Century style shops and Norwest Crossing. A tourist information center here offers brochures, skyway tours and city maps. A skyway connects this area to the City Center.

    WORLD TRADE CENTER and CITY CENTER Eighth St. between Wabasha and Cedar Sts., 297-1580. Clearing house for International Trade. Domed atrium with cascading fountain, shops, offices and restaurants.
15. SCIENCE MUSEUM OF MINNESOTA and the WILLIAM L. McKNIGHT OMNITHEATER 30 E. Tenth St., 221-9400, 221-9488. Science and natural history in a unique museum and a domed screen with a large film projector make these two places a must to see. Tours.
16. ASSUMPTION CHURCH 51 W. Ninth St., 224-7536.
17. CATHEDRAL OF ST. PAUL 239 Selby at Summit Avenue, 225-6563. This exceptionally beautiful cathedral styled after St. Peter's Cathedral in Rome requires a longer walk, but is well worth the effort.

    MINNESOTA HISTORY CENTER 345 Kellogg Boulevard West. Exhibit rooms, reference and research facilities. A beautiful building, and educational experiences. Free. Tours. Cafeteria. 296-6126.

TOUR 4

DOWNTOWN ST. PAUL WALKING TOUR

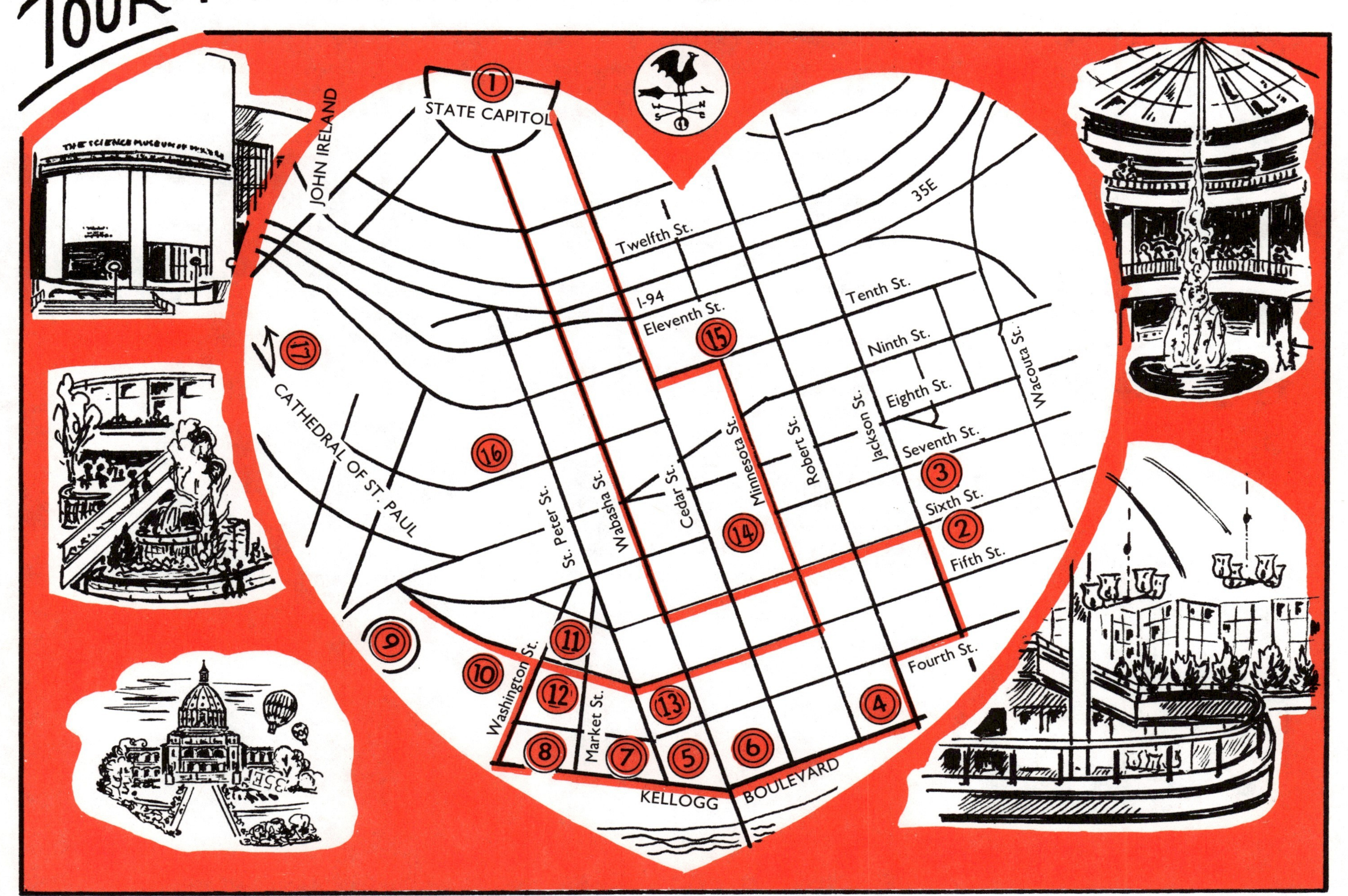

TOUR 5 ST. PAUL PERIMETER SWING

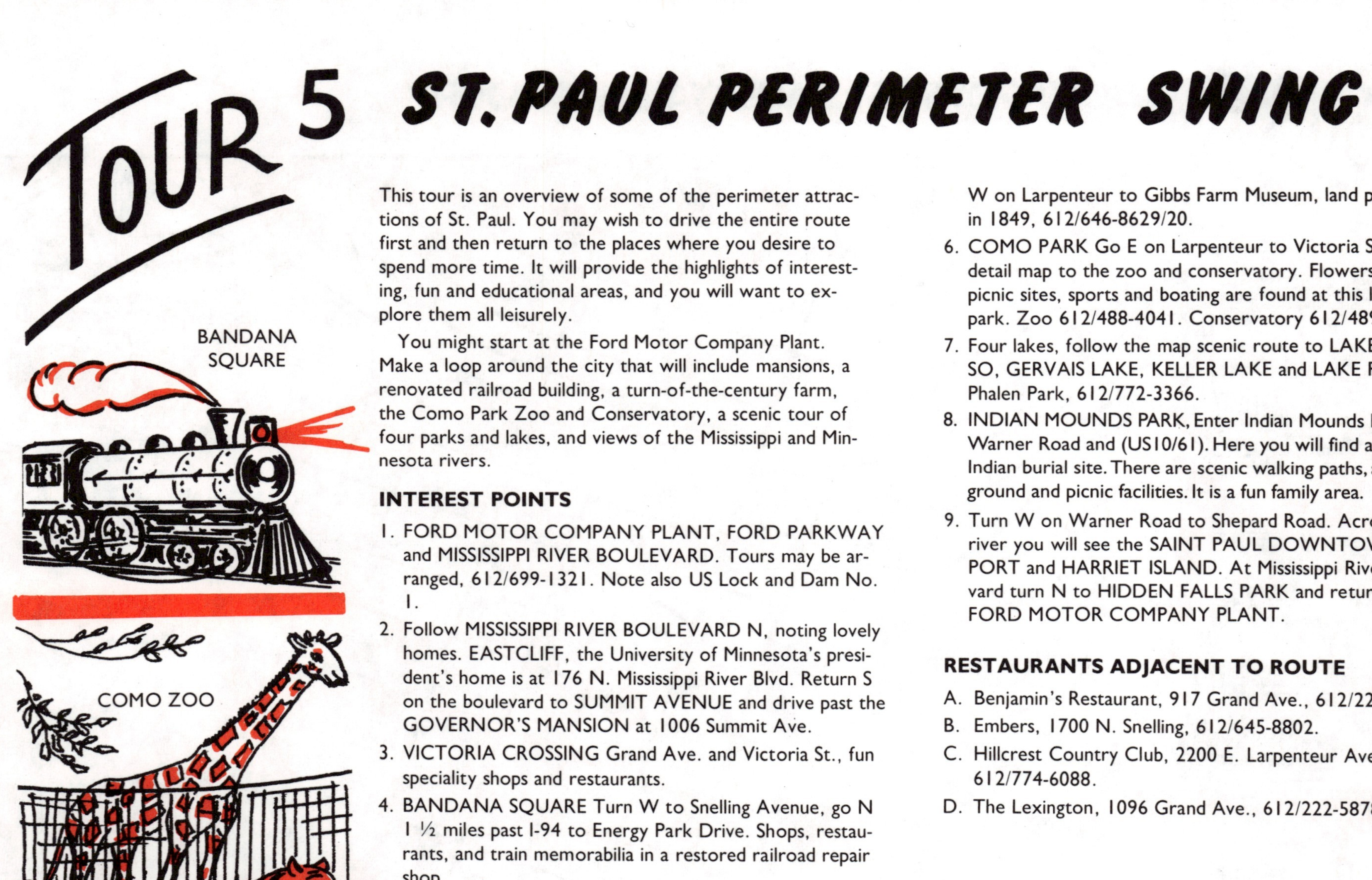

This tour is an overview of some of the perimeter attractions of St. Paul. You may wish to drive the entire route first and then return to the places where you desire to spend more time. It will provide the highlights of interesting, fun and educational areas, and you will want to explore them all leisurely.

You might start at the Ford Motor Company Plant. Make a loop around the city that will include mansions, a renovated railroad building, a turn-of-the-century farm, the Como Park Zoo and Conservatory, a scenic tour of four parks and lakes, and views of the Mississippi and Minnesota rivers.

INTEREST POINTS

1. FORD MOTOR COMPANY PLANT, FORD PARKWAY and MISSISSIPPI RIVER BOULEVARD. Tours may be arranged, 612/699-1321. Note also US Lock and Dam No. 1.
2. Follow MISSISSIPPI RIVER BOULEVARD N, noting lovely homes. EASTCLIFF, the University of Minnesota's president's home is at 176 N. Mississippi River Blvd. Return S on the boulevard to SUMMIT AVENUE and drive past the GOVERNOR'S MANSION at 1006 Summit Ave.
3. VICTORIA CROSSING Grand Ave. and Victoria St., fun speciality shops and restaurants.
4. BANDANA SQUARE Turn W to Snelling Avenue, go N 1 ½ miles past I-94 to Energy Park Drive. Shops, restaurants, and train memorabilia in a restored railroad repair shop.
5. GIBBS FARM MUSEUM 2097 Larpenteur at Cleveland Ave. Drive N on Snelling past the State Fairgrounds. Turn W on Larpenteur to Gibbs Farm Museum, land purchased in 1849, 612/646-8629/20.
6. COMO PARK Go E on Larpenteur to Victoria St., follow detail map to the zoo and conservatory. Flowers, animals, picnic sites, sports and boating are found at this lovely park. Zoo 612/488-4041. Conservatory 612/489-1740.
7. Four lakes, follow the map scenic route to LAKE OWASSO, GERVAIS LAKE, KELLER LAKE and LAKE PHALEN. Phalen Park, 612/772-3366.
8. INDIAN MOUNDS PARK, Enter Indian Mounds Park at Warner Road and (US10/61). Here you will find a historic Indian burial site. There are scenic walking paths, a playground and picnic facilities. It is a fun family area.
9. Turn W on Warner Road to Shepard Road. Across the river you will see the SAINT PAUL DOWNTOWN AIRPORT and HARRIET ISLAND. At Mississippi River Boulevard turn N to HIDDEN FALLS PARK and return to the FORD MOTOR COMPANY PLANT.

RESTAURANTS ADJACENT TO ROUTE

A. Benjamin's Restaurant, 917 Grand Ave., 612/228-1358.
B. Embers, 1700 N. Snelling, 612/645-8802.
C. Hillcrest Country Club, 2200 E. Larpenteur Ave., 612/774-6088.
D. The Lexington, 1096 Grand Ave., 612/222-5878.

TOUR 5 BANDANA SQUARE, GIBBS FARM and a SCENIC LAKE TOUR

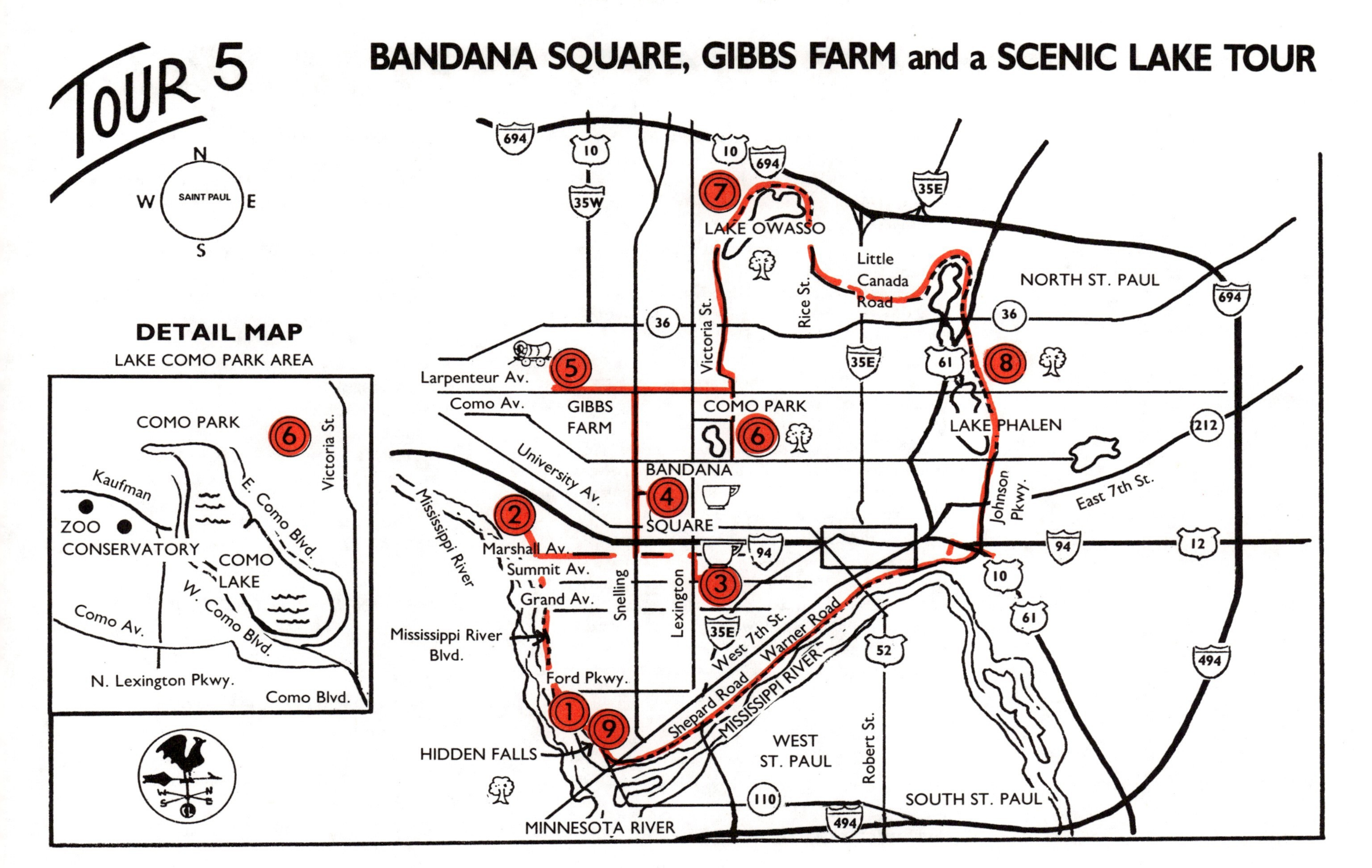

APPROX. TOTAL TOUR MILES 30 — INTEREST POINT — FOOD — HISTORIC SITE — ANTIQUES — PARK — SCENIC ROUTE - - - - — MUSEUM

TOUR 6 A SAILOR DARES TO DREAM

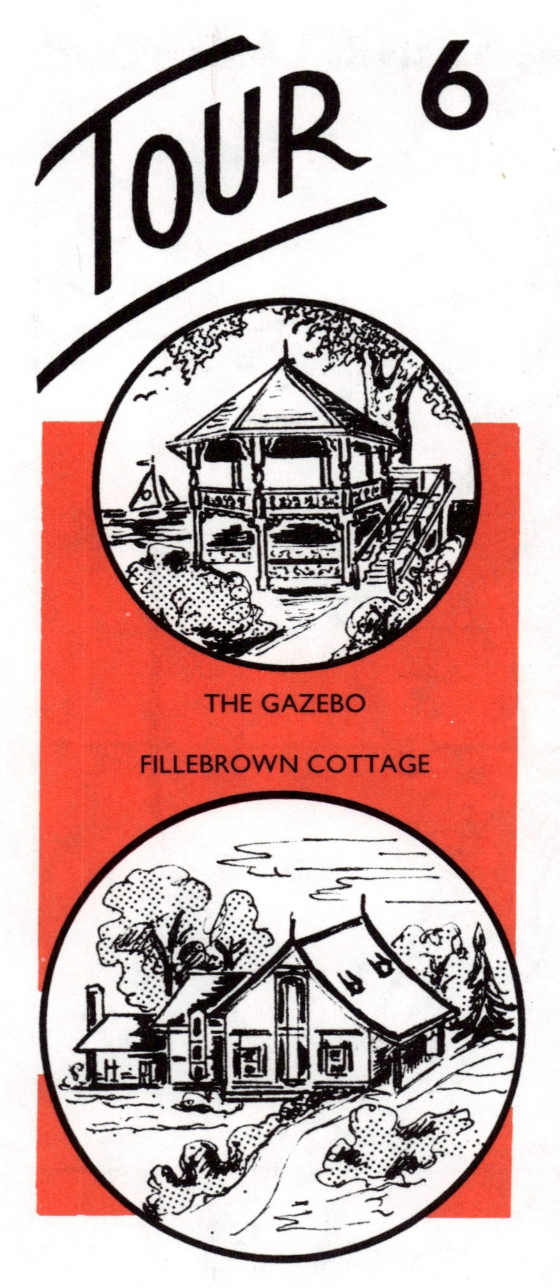

THE GAZEBO

FILLEBROWN COTTAGE

Early in St. Paul's history, White Bear Lake became an elite resort area. The name originated from an Indian legend about a warrior's wife who encountered a monstrous white bear. The warrior slew the bear whose spirit was then believed to dwell in the lake.

Gerry Spiess, who sailed alone in his 11-foot sailboat *Yankee Girl* across both the Atlantic and Pacific oceans, comes from White Bear. The town is a quaint old resort village, so drive or stroll leisurely to savor the special atmosphere of White Bear Lake.

The Fillebrown House, the only remaining cottage, was built in 1879. It has the charming appearance of an old hand-tinted postcard. Walk around it or arrange a tour and imagine what it was like to live here in 1879.

On a walking tour of White Bear you will discover interesting shops that offer custom-blended coffees and teas, handprints in concrete, antiques, chocolates, deli picnic goodies, jewelry and linens.

Follow the tour guidelines to view the interest points. At the north end of the lake you might make a short side trip to the Pine Tree Apple Orchard. Return and make a circle of the lake, continually bearing right. A picnic lunch would be enjoyable in Matoska Park. View the lake from the Gazebo built in 1883. Spiess Landing is named for the town's famous sailor-adventurer. Fine food will be found at local restaurants in the shopping center.

Continue the tour by taking Co. Rd. 96 W to I-35E. Turn N to Co. Rd. 14. Drive through the Chain of Lakes Rice Creek Regional Park. Ramble home through lake-dotted countryside.

INTEREST POINTS

1. SPIESS MARKER in Matoska Park, public landing.
2. THE GAZEBO 4th St. and Lake Ave., built in 1883.
3. MATOSKA PARK 4th St. and Lake Ave.
4. FILLEBROWN HOUSE 1879, 4735 Lake Ave. (corner of Morehead and Lake Avenues, listed in the National Register of Historic Places, open Sunday 1-4 p.m. in summer months or by appointment, 612/426-0479.
5. SOLDIERS' MEMORIAL Clark Ave. and Summit St.
6. TOWNSITE MARKER marks the site and occasion of the dedication of the White Bear Lake Town site in 1871 by the railroad (placed here at the centennial celebration of that occasion).
7. SHOPPING CENTER Restaurant area, many unusual and appealing shops.

   TIMBERDOODLE Historic Building, facing Washington square.
8. JACOBSON'S PINE TREE APPLE ORCHARD Apples, bakery, gifts, honey and syrup, Aug.-Oct. 9 a.m.-9 p.m., Nov.-Jan. 9 a.m.-7 p.m. E on Co. Rd. 96, N on Apple Orchard Rd.
9. CHAIN OF LAKES RICE CREEK REGIONAL PARK at Centerville, Co. Rd. 14 and I-35E.

RESTAURANTS ADJACENT TO ROUTE

A. Holiday House, 1600 Cedar Ave., 612/429-5363.

B. White Bear County Inn, US 61 and MN 96, 612/429-5393.

C. Ruberto's, 1132 E. Co. Rd. E, 612/482-1100.

D. Piccadilly, 70 Mahtomedi Ave., Mahtomedi, 612/426-3455.

White Bear Lake Chamber of Commerce, 613 4th St., White Bear, 612/429-7666.

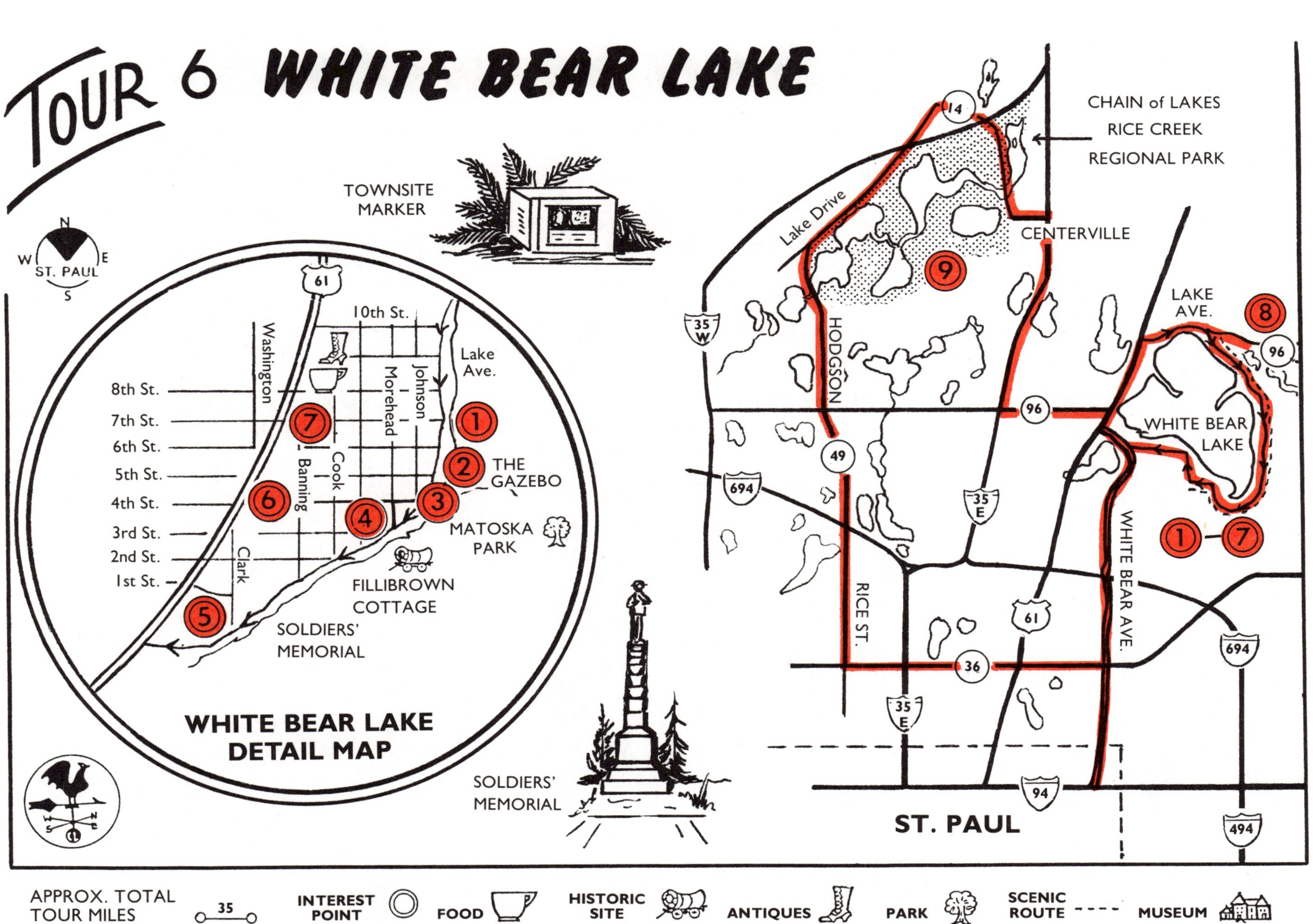

APPROX. TOTAL TOUR MILES 35 | INTEREST POINT | FOOD | HISTORIC SITE | ANTIQUES | PARK | SCENIC ROUTE | MUSEUM

TOUR 7 BUTTERFLY BYWAYS

A LOVELY TOUR

Follow the butterfly-shaped route for a happy day of sightseeing. Learn about area history in the 1888 Fireman's Hall at Cannon Falls. Lake Byllesby is a recreational attraction here. At Zumbrota you will see the only remaining covered bridge in Minnesota used from 1869 to 1932. Read the authentic jackknife carvings made by schoolboys a century ago. Wooden sidewalks are also carved with names.

Red Wing, "Wings of Scarlet" in Dakota, is a delight. Cruise on the *City of Red Wing* on the River, tour the town on the Spirit of Red Wing tram or shop in the three shopping areas. Visit the Goodhue County Historical Museum and the T. B. Sheldon Auditorium. Drive the Memorial Skyline Drive and walk past Victorian homes or hike to Barn Bluff for a sweeping overview.

Cross the Mississippi into Wisconsin and turn right on Co. Rd. 35. Take time to read the rich history as told on the historical markers. Stockholm has an Amish shop you will enjoy. Turn left on Co. Rd. 25 and watch for the Hay Creek Orchard. In Durand, the Durand House Restaurant has windows overlooking the Chippewa River and a bridge. Take US 10 across this bridge, turn on Co. Rd. 25 and follow signs to the Eau Galle Cheese Shop. Return to US 10 and drive through Ellsworth. Turn left on US 63 to Red Wing.

INTEREST POINTS

1. CANNON FALLS Fireman's Hall, 206 Mill St., 1888 Italian-style museum, Lake Byllesby Recreation Area.
2. ZUMBROTA Covered Bridge on US 52, wooden sidewalks.
3. RED WING

   City of Red Wing riverboat cruises, 1758 W. Main, 612/388-7530.

   Spirit of Red Wing Cable Car Co., narrated tours, 612/388-7530.

   Red Wing Pottery Place, Winona Knitting Mills, The Woolen Mill, all on W. Main St.

   Historic homes, ask in local shops for walking tour maps.

   Goodhue County Historical Museum, 1166 Oak St.

   Friedrich Civic Center 5th St. and West Ave.

   T. B. Sheldon Auditorium and Theatre, Third St. at East Avenue, restored to 1904 beauty, 612/388-2806.

   Red Wing Chamber of Commerce, 416 Bush St., 55066, 612/388-4719.
4. HISTORICAL MARKERS on Co. Rd. 35 Bow and Arrow, Maiden Rock and Pepin.
5. STOCKHOLM Amish Shop and Antique Store.
6. DURAND HOUSE RESTAURANT 214 Main St., view of river and bridge, 715/672-5975.
7. EAU GALLE CHEESE SHOP Co. Rd. 25, follow signs.

RESTAURANTS ADJACENT TO ROUTE

A. The Edgewood, 7 miles S of Cannon Falls on US 52, 507/778-3277.

B. Cannonball Cafe, US 52 S., Cannon Falls, 507/263-3396.

C. RED WING

Hardee's, 726 Main St., 612/388-1242.

Liberty's, 3rd and Plum, 612/388-8877.

Larry's Broiler, 915 W. Main, 612/388-6494.

Nybo's Landing, 233 Withers Harbor Dr., 612/388-3597.

The Pantry, 3155 S. Service Dr., 612/388-4419.

The Armory Dining, 3rd and Plum, 612/388-2806.

Bev's Cafe, 221 Bush St., 612/388-5227.

Big Ben Restaurant, 3399 S. Service Dr., 612/388-3269.

St. James Hotel's Port of Red Wing, Veranda Cafe, and Victorian Dining Room, 406 Main St., 612/388-2846.

D. Durand House Restaurant, 214 Main St., Durand, WI, 715/672-5975.

E. Covered Bridge Restaurant, Hwy. 52 N., Zumbrota, 507/732-7321.

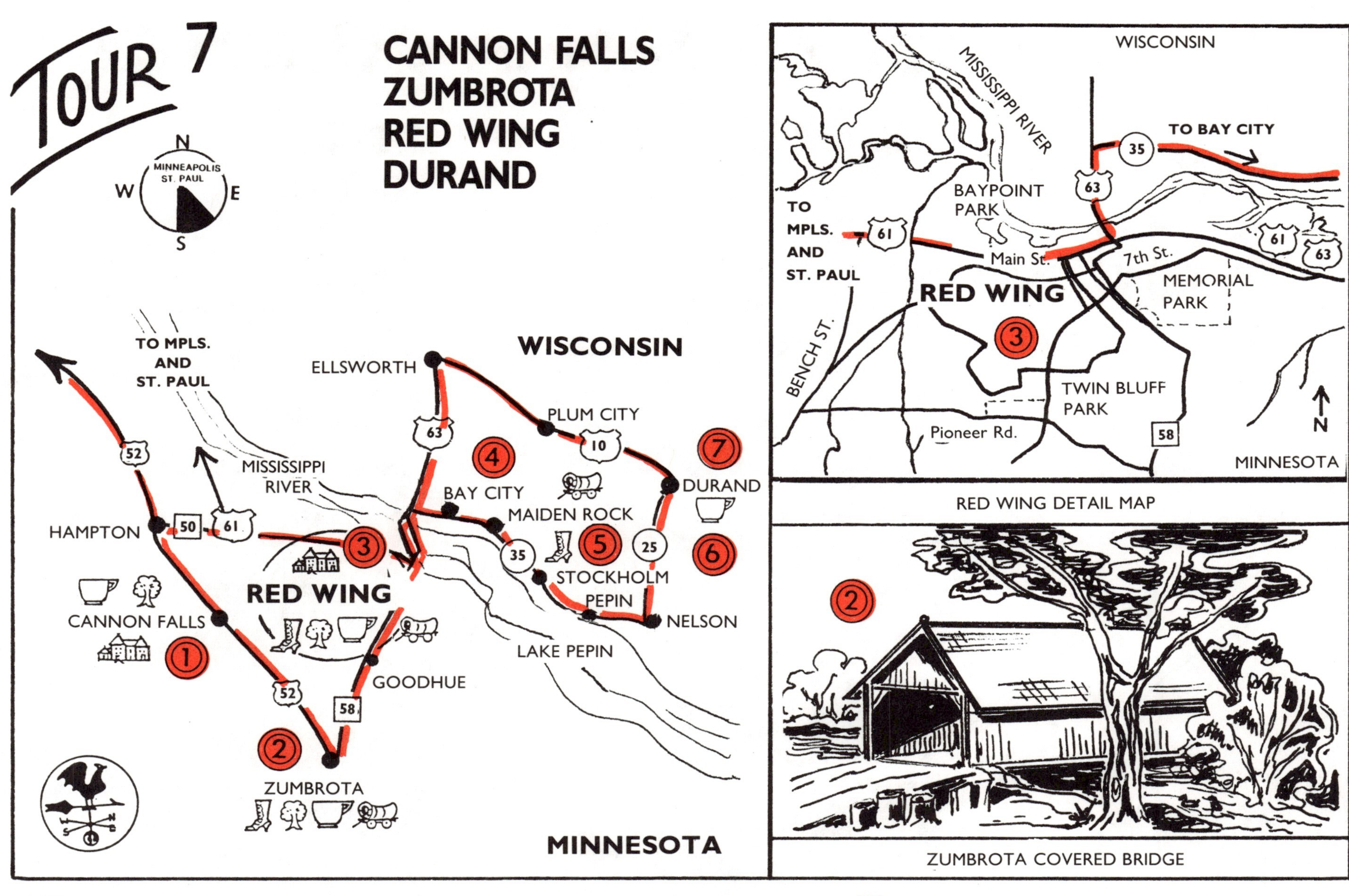

RED WING DETAIL MAP

ZUMBROTA COVERED BRIDGE

APPROX. TOTAL TOUR MILES 185 · INTEREST POINT · FOOD · HISTORIC SITE · ANTIQUES · PARK · SCENIC ROUTE · MUSEUM

TOUR 8 HARBOR COVES AND A CRYSTAL CAVE

CHEESE

APPLES

ST. JOHN'S CHAPEL
MENOMONIE

Quaint river towns and sparkling river and lake water views make this tour a day to remember. There are antiques, museums, state parks, fun shops, historic homes, a flood control dam, scenic farmlands and cheese and apple shops. Beauty all around will make you relax and enjoy the day on this Minnesota and Wisconsin outing.

INTEREST POINTS

1. AFTON Turn S off US 12 on Co. Rd. 95. Here is an old mill site, a Hot Air Balloon Manufacturing Company, Lakeland, Lake St. Croix and St. Mary's Point and marinas galore. In the lovely town of Afton you will discover a pottery, a yarn shop, crafts, toys and giftware.

   AFTON STATE PARK Trails, 2 miles of river frontage high above views of the valley and opportunities for bird-watching make this park an adventure, Park Manager 612/436-5391.

2. HUDSON is situated on the beautiful St. Croix river and, with homes preserved from the past, is a visitor's favorite.

   The OCTAGON HOUSE built in 1855 and furnished with original furniture is a tour spot you will treasure, 1004 Third St., 715/386-2654, tours.

   The CARRIAGE HOUSE MUSEUM and The Indian Mounds are other sites to explore.

   PHIPPS CENTER FOR THE ARTS offers a wide program of Wurlitzer pipe organ concerts, theater, music, arts, dance and fun, 109 Locust St., 715/386-8409.

   WISCONSIN TOURIST INFORMATION CENTER, exit at REST AREA 25 on I-94E.

   BALDWIN The New Leaf Nursery has a Farm Museum. I-94 and Co. Rd. 13, 715/684-2856. At Farm City typical farm life is depicted; contact the St. Croix County Agent for details of Farm City Days, Baldwin, WI 54002.

   Knapp Creamery and Cheese Shop, US 12, right on Co. Rd. 60, left to Creamery, 715/665-2266.

3. SPRING VALLEY Here is the world's highest earthern dam built to avoid disastrous annual flooding of the area. There are two overlooks at the dam site, picnic grounds and lovely Lake Eau Galle.

4. CRYSTAL CAVE One mile S of Spring Valley you will find the turn-off for the caves (note detail map) where a "lost river" formed a geological wonder creation. There are sanded paths and the temperature is 48 degrees the year around. Tours are conducted every 20 minutes and a jacket is necessary. For information call 715/778-4414. Gift shop.

5. MENOMONIE This city 70 miles from the Twin Cities has Lake Menomin.

   CONNELL'S ORCHARD is E of Hudson, WI on I-94 to 128, then S on 128 to Co. Rd. 29, then follow orchard signs. 715/772-4555.

   WILSON PLACE MUSEUM 1859 by Lake Menomonie Bridge has tours, 715/235-2283.

   MABEL TAINTER MEMORIAL BUILDING has a Victorian Theater and tours available, Downtown, 715/235-9726.

   JOHN HOLLY KNAPP HOME (Bundy Hall), 500 Meadow Hills Drive, 715/235-2833.

   ST. JOHN'S IN THE WILDERNESS CHAPEL On the Bundy Hall property, 715/235-9757.

   LIONS CLUB GAME PARK Pine Avenue to Wakanda Park.

6. EAU CLAIRE You may extend this tour for two major attractions.

   FANNY HILL DINNER THEATER Fine food is coupled with a current theater production, Crescent Drive (Co. Rd. EE), 715/836-8184, reservations.

   CHIPPEWA VALLEY MUSEUM Carson Park Drive and Grand Avenue, an exciting link to the past, 76 major exhibits, 715/834-7871.

   ST. CROIX MEADOWS GREYHOUND RACING PARK, 2200 Carmichael Rd., Hudson, Wis. 715/436-5050.

RESTAURANTS ADJACENT TO ROUTE

A. The Afton House, St. Croix Trail and 33rd St., Afton, MN 612/436-8883.

B. The Coachman Restaurant, I-94 and US 63, Baldwin, WI.

TOUR 8

AFTON, HUDSON, SPRING VALLEY AND MENOMONIE

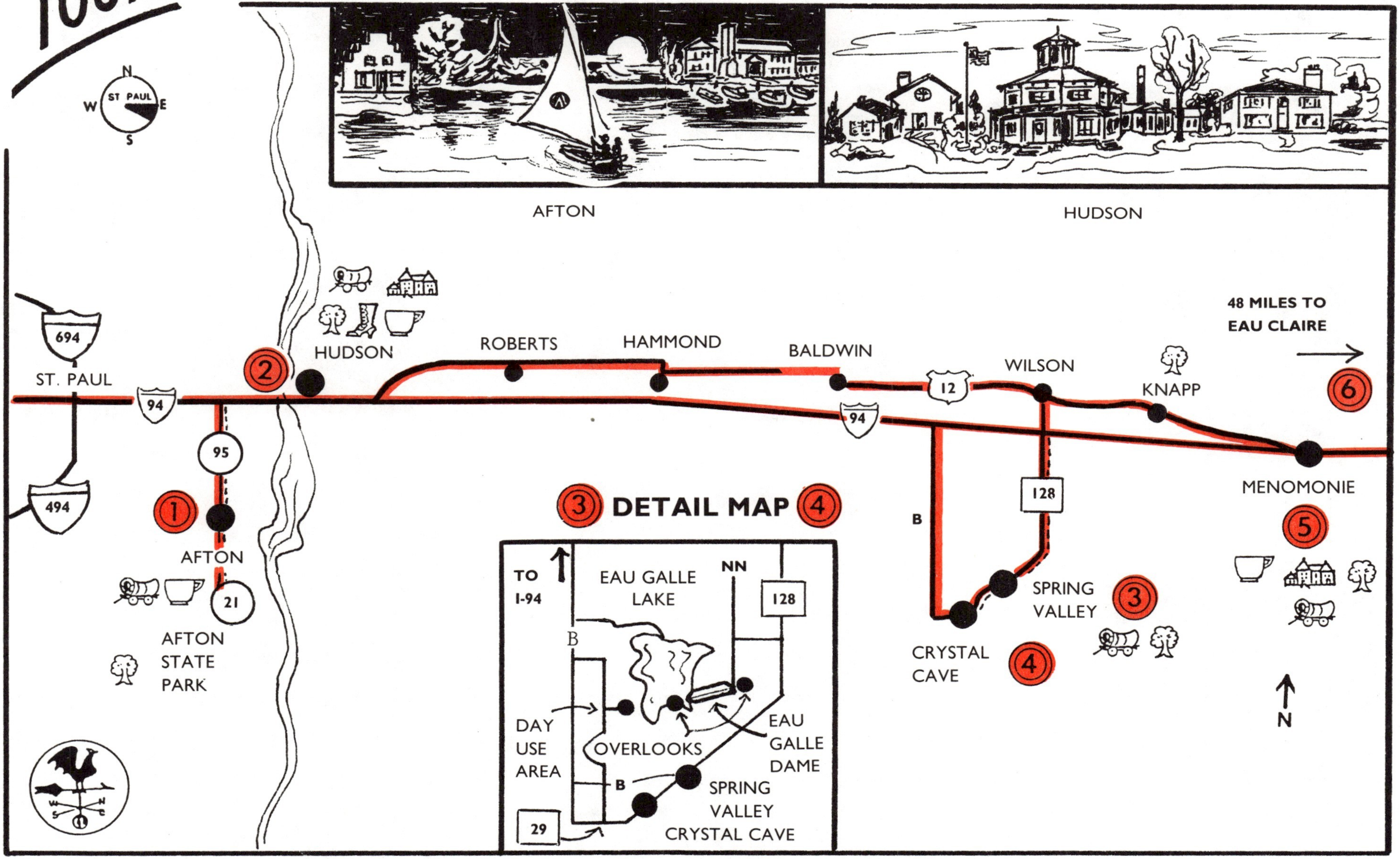

AFTON

HUDSON

694

ST. PAUL

94

2

HUDSON

ROBERTS

HAMMOND

BALDWIN

12

WILSON

KNAPP

48 MILES TO EAU CLAIRE

6

95

494

1

AFTON

21

AFTON STATE PARK

94

128

MENOMONIE

5

B

3 DETAIL MAP 4

TO I-94

EAU GALLE LAKE

NN

128

B

DAY USE AREA

OVERLOOKS

EAU GALLE DAME

B

SPRING VALLEY

CRYSTAL CAVE

29

SPRING VALLEY

3

CRYSTAL CAVE

4

N

APPROX. TOTAL TOUR MILES 140

INTEREST POINT

FOOD

HISTORIC SITE

ANTIQUES

PARK

SCENIC ROUTE

MUSEUM

TOUR 9

METRO MINNEAPOLIS

FOSHAY TOWER
FIRST MINNEAPOLIS
TALL BUILDING

WELCOME TO MINNEAPOLIS

An exciting way to explore the ins and outs of the bright and bustling city of Minneapolis is to take a street-level walking tour of the downtown area. Imposing buildings tower above the well-known Nicollet Mall. Here urban activity flourishes in a setting of trees, fountains, flowers and seasonal decor.

As the tour is followed, street facades and inner attractions delight the stroller. You will discover the multi-purpose library, department stores and specialty shops, atriums and glass-crowned courts, government facilities, grain exchange procedures, an impressive metrodome, a modern convention center, a lovely jewel lake in a park, art museums, a sculpture garden, cloud-touching skyscrapers—all these within easy walking distance.

1. MINNEAPOLIS PUBLIC LIBRARY and PLANETARIUM 300 Nicollet Mall, varied services, the sculpture "The Scroll" at East entrance, tours, 612/372-6667.

   THE NICOLLET MALL begins here, the nation's longest urban pedestrian stroll-way that is appealing in all seasons.
2. HENNEPIN CENTER FOR THE ARTS 528 Hennepin Ave., ornate exterior architecture, art interests, 612/332-4478
3. BUTLER SQUARE 100 N. 6th St., restored warehouse with beamed atrium and office and specialty shops, 612/339-4343.

   TARGET CENTER, 600 First Ave. N, 612/673-1300.
4. CITY CENTER 33 S. 7th St., shops and restaurants facing an open atrium, 612/372-1580.
5. IDS CENTER 80 S. 8th St., 57-story building and activity center, visitor information, 120-foot high magnificent crystal court, balcony restaurants have court view, 612/372-1660.
6. THE CONSERVATORY 808 Nicollet Mall, granite and glass exterior and curving interior stairway, 612/322-4649.
7. ORCHESTRA HALL 1111 Nicollet Mall, home of the Minnesota Orchestra, 612/371-5600.
8. LORING GREENWAY LaSalle at 13th., leads to lovely LORING PARK, GUTHRIE THEATER, WALKER ART CENTER and the exciting SCULPTURE GARDEN.

   THE BASILICA OF ST. MARY is south on Hennepin at 16th St. Tours, 612/333-1381.
9. THE MINNEAPOLIS AUDITORIUM and CONVENTION CENTER Grant at Second Ave., vitally new in a resplendent pink and blue-green color duo, 612/870-4436.
10. FOSHAY TOWER 821 Marquette Ave., a landmark designed after the Washington Monument, 612/341-2522.
11. LUTHERAN BROTHERHOOD 625 4th Ave. S., unusual design, tours, 612/340-7054.
12. HENNEPIN COUNTY GOVERNMENT CENTER between 3rd and 4th Avenues on S 7th St., twin towers, observation bridge on 23rd floor, 612/348-3190.
13. MINNEAPOLIS CITY HALL 350 S. 5th St., 612/348-3000.
14. HUBERT H. HUMPHREY METRODOME 900 S. 5th St., dramatic climate-controlled dome, tours, 612/332-0386.
15. RIVER CITY TROLLEY, Discover historic Minneapolis—take the River City Trolley. Call for starting points, 612/204-0000.

Watch for these tall buildings as you walk:

IDS CENTER 80 S. 8th St., 57 stories, 776 feet high.
NORWEST CENTER Sixth and Marquette Avenue, 57 stories, 772.5 feet high.
MULTIFOODS TOWER 33 S. 6th St., 52 stories, 608 feet high.
PIPER JAFFRAY TOWER 222 S. 9th St., 42 stories, 580.5 feet high.
OPUS 150 S. 5th St., 36 stories, 503 feet high.
PLAZA VII 45 S. 7th St., 36 stories, 475 feet high.
PILLSBURY CENTER 200 S. 6th St., 42 stories, 561 feet high.
AT&T 8th St. and Marquette Ave., 34 stories.
Lincoln Centre 333 S. 7th St., 32 stories, 454 feet high.
FOSHAY TOWER 821 Marquette Avenue S., 32 stories, 447.2 feet high.

TOUR 9 DOWNTOWN MINNEAPOLIS WALKING TOUR

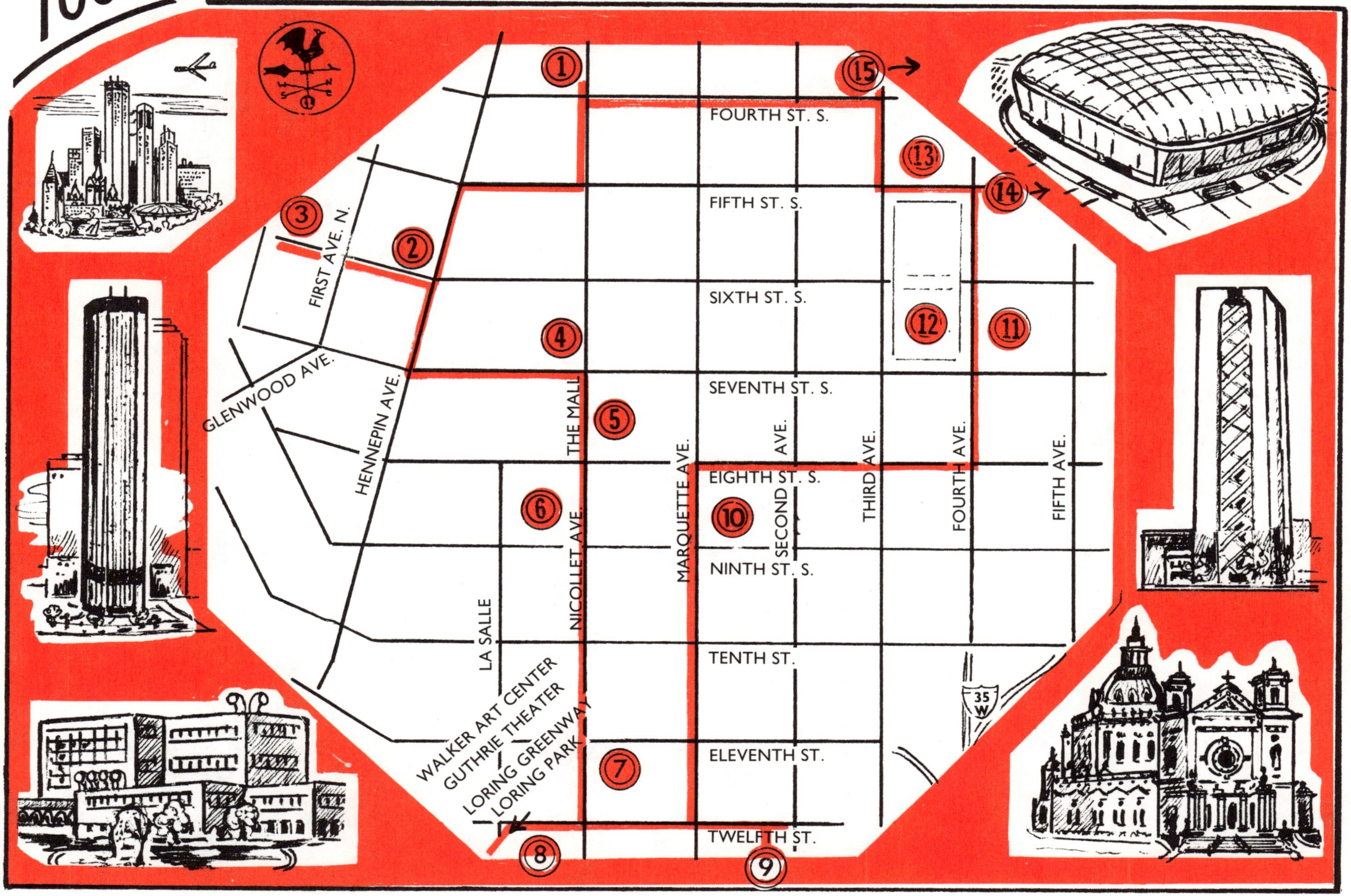

FOURTH ST. S.
FIFTH ST. S.
SIXTH ST. S.
SEVENTH ST. S.
EIGHTH ST. S.
NINTH ST. S.
TENTH ST.
ELEVENTH ST.
TWELFTH ST.
FIRST AVE. N.
GLENWOOD AVE.
HENNEPIN AVE.
THE MALL
NICOLLET AVE.
LA SALLE
MARQUETTE AVE.
SECOND AVE.
THIRD AVE.
FOURTH AVE.
FIFTH AVE.
35 W
WALKER ART CENTER
GUTHRIE THEATER
LORING GREENWAY
LORING PARK
1 2 3 4 5 6 7 8 9 10 11 12 13 14 15

TOUR 10 DISCOVER THE UNUSUAL

How many of the following Twin City attractions are you familiar with? Have you explored them on a tour, not just driven past or seen a photograph? Take a quiz to determine your knowledge. Check only those places that you really know.

1. FIRE FIGHTERS MEMORIAL MUSEUM Magnificent antique equipment, tours, 1100 N.E. Van Buren St., Minneapolis, 612/623-3817.
2. PAVEK MUSEUM OF WONDERFUL WIRELESS Excellent collection of wireless memorabilia, tours, 3515-17 Raleigh Avenue, St. Louis Park, 612/926-8198.
3. ISLANDS OF PEACE Lovely setting on the river, handicap accessible, interpretive center, 200 Charles St. N.E., Fridley, 612/757-3920.
4. MINNESOTA VALLEY NATIONAL WILDLIFE REFUGE Interpretive center, trails, 4101 E. 80th St., Bloomington, 612/854-5900.
5. MINNESOTA HARVEST ORCHARD Apples and more, Old US 169 at Apple Lover's Lane, Jordan, 612/492-2785.
6. NEW GREAT RIVER ROAD Paths, picnic sites, Portland Ave. to Broadway on the Mississippi River.
7. ANSON NORTHRUP RIVERBOAT EXCURSIONS Boom Island Dock, 612/348-2226.
8. NOERENBERG MEMORIAL GARDENS Gazebo, garden tours, 2840 N. Shore Dr., Wayzata, 612/476-4666.
9. ANTIQUES, MINNESOTA 80 dealers, 1516 E. Lake St., 612/722-6000.
10. THE STREETCAR BOAT MINNEHAHA, Minnehaha Dock, Lake Minnetonka, May 26-Sept. 15. 612/474-4801.
11. AAMODT'S APPLE FARM Restored 1880s barn, 6428 Manning Ave., N., Stillwater, 612/439-3127.
12. CASS GILBERT MEMORIAL PARK Observation lookout, 750 N. Cedar St., St. Paul.
13. PAYNE AVENUE ANTIQUEMALL 50 dealers, 1055 Payne Avenue, St. Paul, 612/772-1635.
14. MINNESOTA AIR GUARD MUSEUM Exhibits, hangar tours, Minneapolis-St. Paul International Airport/Air National Guard Base, 62nd St., and Hiawatha Ave., 612/725-5609.
15. KUEMPEL CHIME CLOCK WORKS Hand-crafted clocks, tours, 21195 Minnetonka Blvd., Excelsior, 612/474-6177.
16. ORIGINAL BASEBALL MUSEUM OF MINNESOTA and R. C. PROMOTION CO. Baseball artifacts and goods, 406-10 Chicago Ave. S., Minneapolis, 612/375-0428.
17. MINNEAPOLIS FIRE STATION # 6 Unusual building design, tours, 121 E. 15th St., 612/874-8691.
18. NORMANDALE JAPANESE GARDENS Shrine, lagoon, tours, 98th St. and France Ave. S., Bloomington, 612/830-9303.
19. BROOKLYN PARK HISTORICAL FARM 10-acre living record, tours, 4345 101st Ave. N., Brooklyn Park, 612/424-8017.
20. ST. ANTHONY UPPER LOCK and DAM # 1 Observation deck, river and city views, old stone bridge, 1 Portland Ave., Minneapolis, 612/333-5336.
21. HYLAND LAKE PARK RESERVE Chutes and ladders hillside play area, picnic shelter, trails, 10145 E. Bush Lake Rd., Bloomington, 612/941-4362.
22. MINNEAPOLIS SCULPTURE GARDEN Vineland Place, 612/375-7600.
23. LAKE CORNELIA PARK Pool, picnic shelter, trails, W. 66th St. and Valley View Rd., Edina, 612/927-9829.
24. THE WABASHA AVENUE CAVES, 215 S. Wabasha St., St. Paul. 612/224-1191.
25. WEALTHY APPLE ORIGIN Seed development history plaque, Co. Rd. 19 (across from NSP), Navarre.

Count your quiz score by adding four points for each correct answer. 72-100: excellent, you must be proud of the area where you live. 48-72: good, you've tried to get around the towns. 32-48: well, you are not too knowledgeable, right? 16-32: you would be a poor person to ask directions of. 0-16: better start with any tour in the book and take the family, friends or a group tour to see these interesting places. It's fun to get to know our exciting Twin Cities area.

TOUR 10

DO YOU KNOW THESE TWIN CITY PLACES?

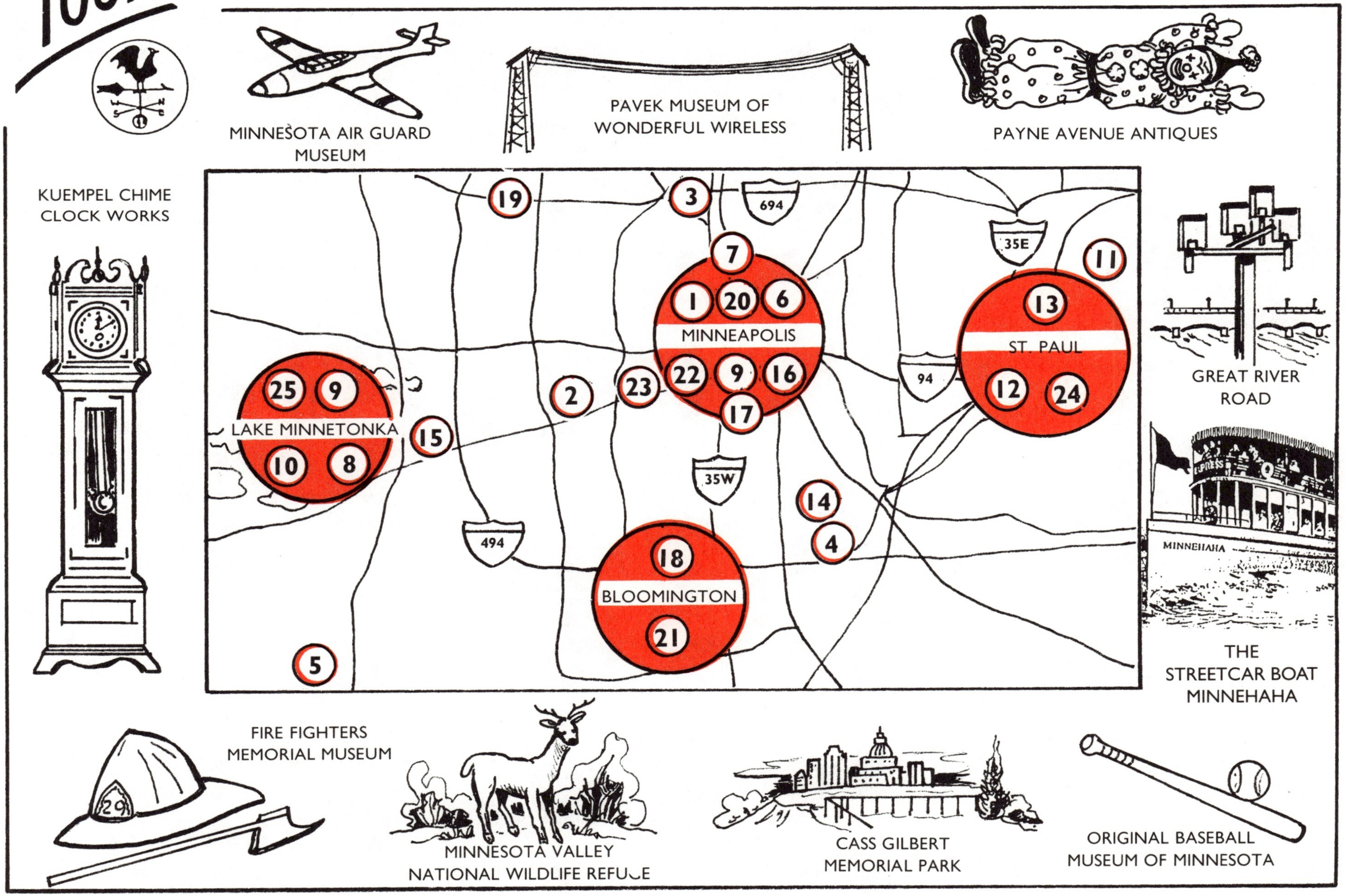

MINNESOTA AIR GUARD MUSEUM

PAVEK MUSEUM OF WONDERFUL WIRELESS

PAYNE AVENUE ANTIQUES

KUEMPEL CHIME CLOCK WORKS

694

35E

19

3

7

11

1

20

6

MINNEAPOLIS

13

ST. PAUL

22

9

16

94

12

24

25

9

2

23

17

LAKE MINNETONKA

15

10

8

35W

14

494

18

4

BLOOMINGTON

21

5

GREAT RIVER ROAD

MINNEHAHA

THE STREETCAR BOAT MINNEHAHA

FIRE FIGHTERS MEMORIAL MUSEUM

29

MINNESOTA VALLEY NATIONAL WILDLIFE REFUGE

CASS GILBERT MEMORIAL PARK

ORIGINAL BASEBALL MUSEUM OF MINNESOTA

TOUR 11 MAJESTIC MINNETONKA

NOERENBERG MEMORIAL GARDEN AND GAZEBO

SITE WHERE WEALTHY APPLES WERE DEVELOPED

Lake Minnetonka, with 120 miles of shoreline, is a beautiful tour. Soldiers stationed at Ft. Snelling explored Minnehaha Creek to its source at Grays Bay in 1822. When the railroad came in 1857, famous hotels and steamboats were plentiful. Homes and towns soon lined the shores. Excelsior and Big Island (which had a lighthouse) drew vacationing crowds. Sinclair Lewis, Elliot Roosevelt, Westbrook Pegler and Adlai Stevenson all were resident here at one time.

You will see quaint shops, marinas, channels and bridges. Fine eating places include a dinner-train ride, a dinner-water cruise and a dinner-theater.

INTEREST POINTS

1. THE GENERAL STORE Handcrafted goods, 14401 MN 7, one-half mi. W of I-494, 612/935-2215.

   Note historic Oak Hill Cemetery as you enter Excelsior.
2. THE OLD LOG THEATER Lunch or dinner, live drama, 5175 Meadville St., Excelsior, 612/474-5951.
3. KUEMPEL CHIME CLOCK WORKS Clock craft shop, tours, 21195 Minnetonka Blvd., 612/474-6177.
4. EXCELSIOR Places of special interest include: Main Street with antique and specialty shops.

   CHRISTOPHER INN bed and breakfast in a restored historic house, 201 Mill St., 612/474-6460.

   TRINITY EPISCOPAL CHURCH 1862, 300 Second St.

   LADY-OF-THE-LAKE boat cruises Old Excelsior Boat Dock, 612/929-1209.

   QUEEN OF EXCELSIOR charter dinner-cruises, 612/474-2502.

   THE STREETCAR BOAT MINNEHAHA, Lake Minnetonka, Ride the STEAMBOAT, 612/474-4801.

   THE COMMONS park, swimming and picnic at lakeside.
5. Site where the Wealthy apple was developed. Marker tells the history, on Co. Rd. 19 (across from NSP).
6. SPRING PARK is the departure point for the HIAWATHA DINNER TRAIN, 612/471-7811.

   LANGDON BAY TRADING POST Antiques and collectables, Co. Rds. 15 and 110, Mound, 612/472-4433.
7. NOERENBERG MEMORIAL GARDENS and GAZEBO Tours available. 2840 N. Shore Dr., Wayzata, 612/476-4666.
8. LONG LAKE AREA MUSEUM 1953 Wayzata Blvd., Long Lake, tours available, 612/473-6557.
9. WAYZATA Village shops and antiques, Old Depot built by James J. Hill, 1906.
10. MINNEHAHA CREEK originates in wetland area off Co. Rd 16.
11. BURWELL HOUSE Historic home built on the site of the first flour mill W of the Mississippi, tours available, E. of I-494 on Co. Rd. 16, 612/933-2511.

RESTAURANTS ADJACENT TO ROUTE

A. Mai Tai, 687 Excelsior Blvd., Excelsior, 612/474-1183.

B. Copper Stein Restaurant, 5635 Manitou Rd., Excelsior, 612/474-5805.

C. Mamalu's BBQ, I-494 and MN 7, Minnetonka, 612/933-3663.

D. Perkins Family Restaurant, 17701 MN 7, Minnetonka, 612/474-2568.

E. Al and Alma's, 5201 Piper Rd., Mound, 612/472-3098.

F. Lord Fletchers of the Lake, 3746 Sunset Dr., Spring Park, 612/471-8513.

G. Minnetonka Mist, 4050 Shoreline Dr., Spring Park, 612/471-8471.

H. Muffuletta on the Lake, 739 E. Lake St., Wayzata, 612/475-3636.

Other restaurants will be found at:

Bonaventure, US 12 and Plymouth Rd., 612/591-0264.

Ridgedale, 12401 Wayzata Blvd., 612/922-1938.

Knollwood Mall, 8332 MN 7, 612/933-8041.

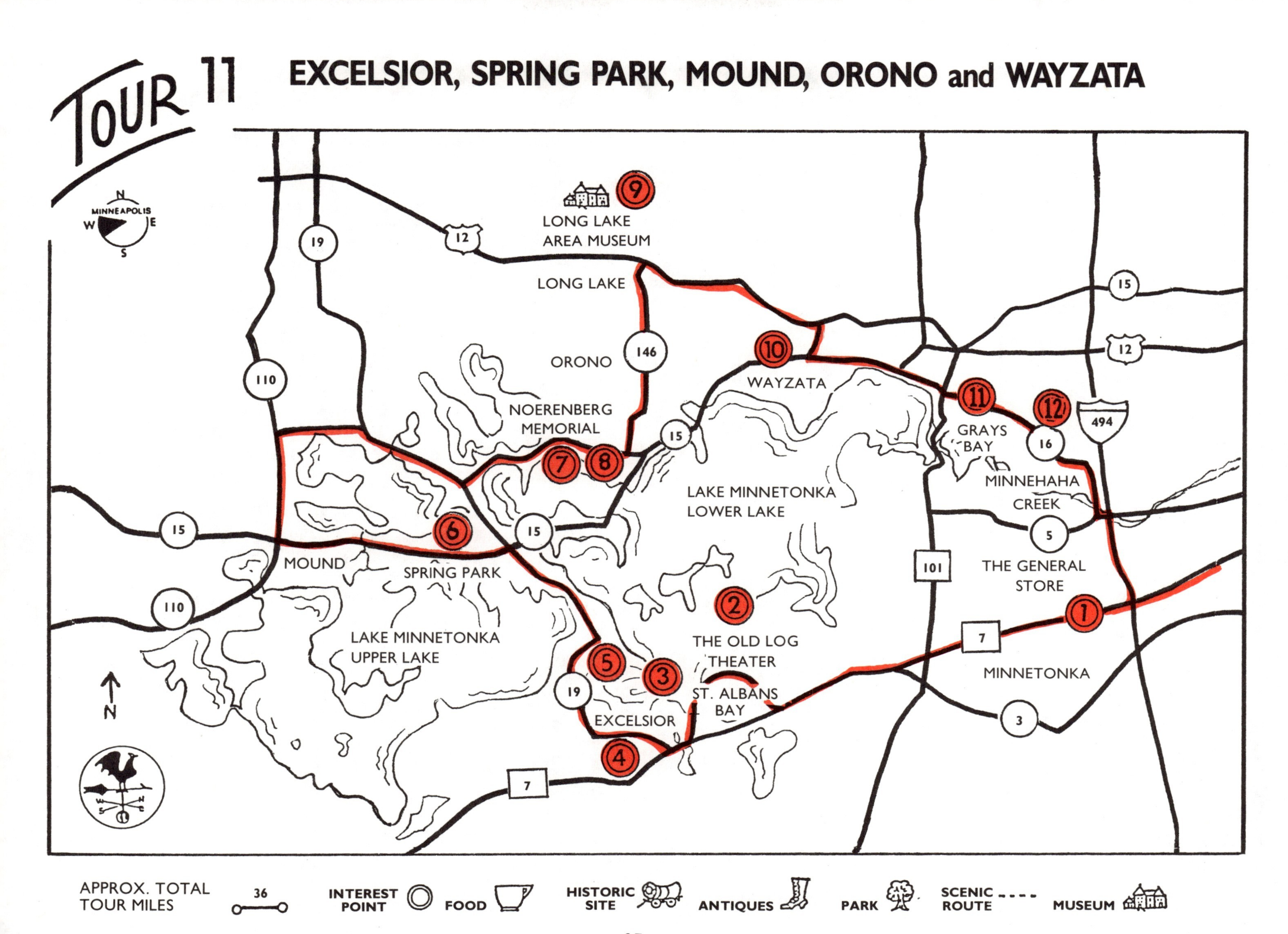
TOUR 11
EXCELSIOR, SPRING PARK, MOUND, ORONO and WAYZATA
N
MINNEAPOLIS
W
E
S
19
12
9
LONG LAKE
AREA MUSEUM
LONG LAKE
15
146
ORONO
110
10
WAYZATA
12
NOERENBERG
MEMORIAL
11
12
494
GRAYS
BAY
16
15
7
8
LAKE MINNETONKA
LOWER LAKE
MINNEHAHA
CREEK
15
6
15
5
MOUND
SPRING PARK
101
THE GENERAL
STORE
110
2
1
LAKE MINNETONKA
UPPER LAKE
THE OLD LOG
THEATER
7
MINNETONKA
5
3
19
ST. ALBANS
BAY
EXCELSIOR
3
N
4
7
APPROX. TOTAL
TOUR MILES
36
INTEREST
POINT
FOOD
HISTORIC
SITE
ANTIQUES
PARK
SCENIC
ROUTE
MUSEUM

TOUR 12 SUBURBAN SECRETS FUN TO EXPLORE

MINNESOTA ZOOLOGICAL GARDEN

To really get to know an area, leave the highway and follow the byroads and farm roads. Such country roads just outside the Cities are found in a nearby location not often thought of for discovery. Here are clusters of lakes, a zoo, an air traffic control facility and an 1,170-foot hill with I-35W at its foot. Open farm lands remain, although they are surrounded by rapid development. You will note that this is horse country where thoroughbreds are raised. Burnsville, west of I-35W, is included in Tour 1.

INTEREST POINTS

1. BURNSVILLE FANTASUITE HOTEL, 250 North River Ridge Circle, Burnsville 612/890-9550.
2. DIAMONDHEAD MALL Specialty shops, handcrafts, two blocks E of I-35W on Burnsville Parkway.
3. BURNSVILLE CENTER Several levels of shops, I-35W and MN 42.
4. CRYSTAL LAKE PARK From the Burnsville Center drive S on the west service road (Crystal Lake Rd.), cross the bridge over I-35W and you will come to scenic parks on Crystal Lake. Return to the west service road and turn S onto Buck Hill Road.
5. BUCK HILL SKI AREA Even in summer this is an interesting place to see, 15000 Buck Hill Rd., 612/435-7187. Adjacent to the ski area, just north are the BEAVER MOUNTAIN WATER SLIDES.
6. LAKEVILLE Follow Buck Hill Road to MN 50 and turn left. SOUTH FORK CENTER is here. At 201st St. turn right into ANTLER'S PARK with picnic sites.
7. FARMINGTON South of MN 50 and Co. Rd. 3 turn W and look for a tall antenna. Here is the Minneapolis Air Route Traffic Control; tours are available and it is amazing to watch the huge screens and the operators who guide the airplanes into the main airport, 612/726-5574.
8. EMPIRE At 200th St. and US 52 is a small river which formerly ran grist mills in pioneer days. There are thoroughbred stables in this area, and the Vermillion barns allowed our group to tour the buildings, 612/437-8485.
9. ROSEMOUNT Dakota County Vo-Tech is W of US 52 and MN 42. Tours are interesting, 612/423-2281.
10. THE COUNTRY STORE A collector's joy with handcrafted items for your browsing pleasure, 12000 S. Robert Trail (Co. Rd. 3), 612/423-1242.
11. EAGAN Lebanon Hills Regional Park has several lakes and varied activity choices.
12. SCHERER GARDENS are lovely formal gardens with roses, streams and bridges to delight the eye and the camera. Donations only for self-guided tours, 1535 Cliff Rd., 612/454-4521.
13. MINNESOTA ZOOLOGICAL GARDENS are open all year and five trails exhibit 1,300 animals and 800 plant species. Admission, senior discount and parking extra, 12101 Johnny Cake Ridge Rd., 612/431-9200.

    Take MN 42 to Cedar Avenue (Co. Rd. 77) then N to Cliff Road to return to starting point of tour.

RESTAURANTS ADJACENT TO ROUTE

A. J.R. Maxmillian's in the Burnsville Fantasuite Hotel, 250 North River Ridge Circle, Burnsville Circle, Burnsville, 612/890-9550.

B. Old Country Buffet, 14150 Nicollet, Burnsville, 612/435-6511.

C. Farmington Steak House, 329 3rd St., Farmington, 612/463-3726.

D. House of Coates, US 52, Coates, 612/437-2232.

E. Denny's. 2400 Cliff Road and Co. Rd. 13, Eagan, 612/894-5583.

F. Durning's, 4625 Nicols Road, (Cedar Ave. and Cliff Rd.), Eagan, 612/454-6744.

TOUR 12

BURNSVILLE, EAGAN, ROSEMOUNT, APPLE VALLEY, FARMINGTON, LAKEVILLE and EMPIRE

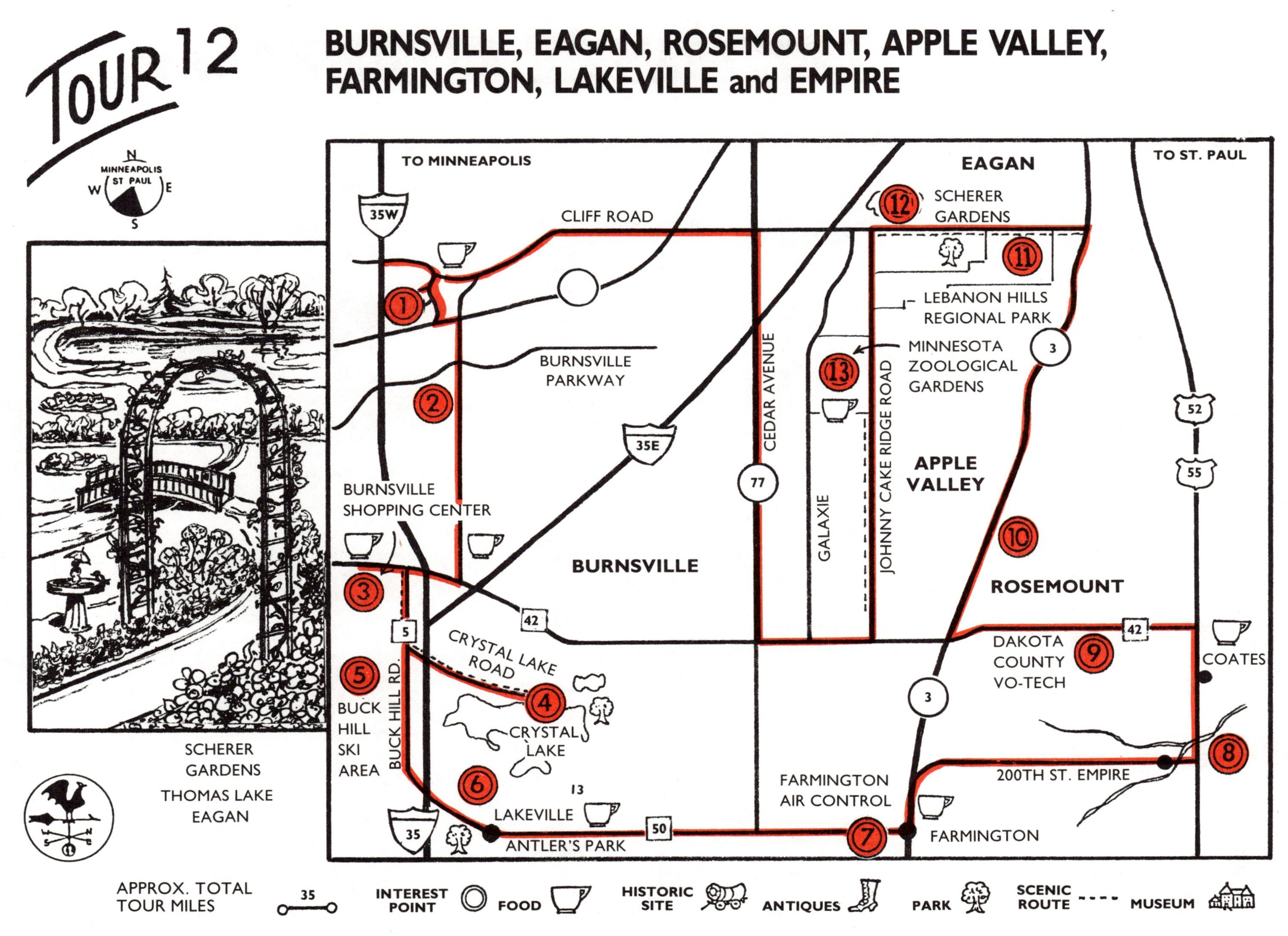

SCHERER
GARDENS
THOMAS LAKE
EAGAN

APPROX. TOTAL TOUR MILES 35 — INTEREST POINT — FOOD — HISTORIC SITE — ANTIQUES — PARK — SCENIC ROUTE — MUSEUM

TOUR 13 MANSIONS AND STEAMBOATS

VERMILLION FALLS
HASTINGS

Mansions and steamboats offer a turn-of-the-century way to brighten a tour. This route meanders through both the Minnesota and the Wisconsin sides of the Mississippi River. The Great River Road begins here with an assurance of interest and beauty. River towns are framed by the bluffs. It is easy to conjure an image of the steamboats that once brought supplies and carried the settlers who found a new homeland here. Later mansions were built as lumbering and mills made enterprising leaders prosperous. The first iron bridge in the state was built in Hastings to carry railroad trains over the Mississippi.

INTEREST POINTS

1. HASTINGS Three rivers converge at Hastings, the Mississippi, the St. Croix and the Vermillion. The name Hastings was drawn from a hat (General Henry Hastings Sibley).

   WALKING TOUR OF HASTINGS Inquire at the Hastings Area Chamber of Commerce, 427 Vermillion St., for a map for a walking tour which includes the historic downtown area, historic homes and fine antique shops, 612/437-6775.

   VERMILLION FALLS AND PARK You will find this cascading falls next to a historic mill, Mill and 2nd Sts.

   LOCK and DAM #2 OBSERVATION DECK On Lock and Dam Road.

   REBECCA PARK Adjacent to the Lock and Dam.

   LEDUC-SIMMONS MANSION At Vermillion and 17th Sts., open by appointment only, fee, 612/437-4052.

   CARPENTER NATURE CENTER Environmental education for groups or others on a trail that follows the St. Croix River, 612/437-4359, 12805 St. Croix Trail.

   APPLE ORCHARDS Many apple orchards dot the Hastings area. Watch for roadside signs.

   DAKOTA COUNTY COURTHOUSE 3rd and Vermillion Sts., 612/437-6775.

2. PRESCOTT Situated at the junction of the St. Croix and the Mississippi rivers, this town is picturesque with marinas and boats, a true river city, and was named for Philander Prescott, a fur trader and Indian language interpreter. Early history is romantic with steamboats, immigration and logging operations.

   BROAD STREET View architecture remaining from 1860s and 70s, interesting shops, antiques, a bakery with home-style goodies, and rest spots with views of the river and water activity.

   PRESCOTT LIFT BRIDGE On the site where the first ferry operated, this bridge was built in 1923 and was originally a toll bridge, Broad and Cherry Sts.

   LAKE ST. CROIX Formed partially by sediment from the Mississippi River, this river now extends for miles to form a natural recreation area.

   ST. JOSEPH'S CATHOLIC CHURCH 1912 Twin-domed steeples tower above the downtown. The original church was built on this site in 1868.

   RIVER CRUISES Departing from the Steamboat Inn, enjoyable scenic river cruises are available. Call River Charters, 612/636-2886.

3. COTTAGE GROVE The special attraction is the Cedarhurst Mansion, 6940 Keats Ave. S.: the original part was built in 1860 and later remodeling changes included the addition of the ballroom wing. There are 3 fireplaces, 9 bathrooms, a 100-foot veranda and an elevator. The ballroom has a 18-rank theater pipe organ. Tours are every Tuesday 11 a.m. and 1 p.m.; reservations required for the buffet lunch served at noon, 612/459-9741.

RESTAURANTS ADJACENT TO ROUTE

A. The Chateau, Junction of US 55 and Co. Rd. 52, Inver Grove Heights, MN, 612/437-6663.

B. Mississippi Belle, 101 E. 2nd St., Hastings, MN, 612/427-5694.

C. Weiderholt's Supper Club, 14535 240th St. E., Hastings, MN, 612/437-3528.

D. Perkins, 1206 Vermillion St., Hastings, MN, 612/437-5028.

E. Hardee's, 1309 Vermillion St., Hastings, MN, 612/437-4145.

F. Steamboat Inn, US 10, Prescott, WI, 715/262-1644.

TOUR 13 HASTINGS, PRESCOTT and COTTAGE GROVE

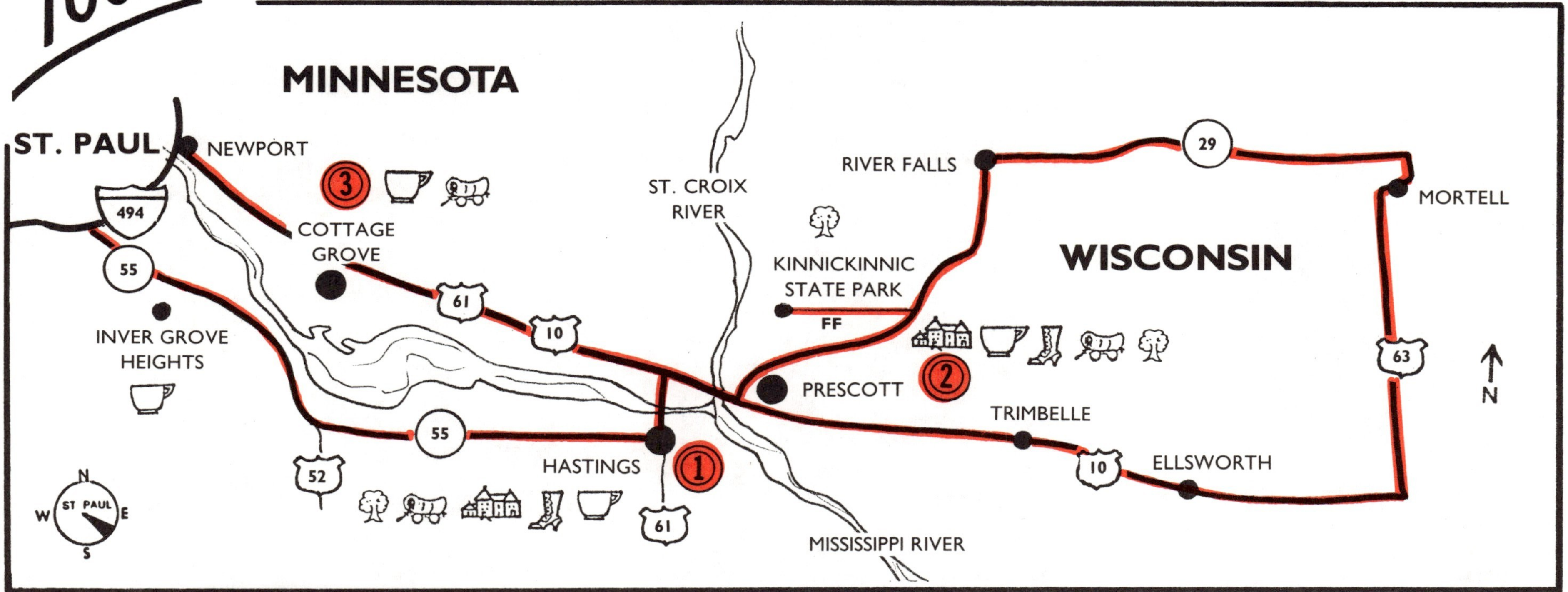

MINNESOTA
ST. PAUL
NEWPORT
494
COTTAGE GROVE
55
INVER GROVE HEIGHTS
61
10
ST. CROIX RIVER
RIVER FALLS
29
MORTELL
KINNICKINNIC STATE PARK
FF
WISCONSIN
PRESCOTT
TRIMBELLE
63
N
55
HASTINGS
52
61
10
ELLSWORTH
MISSISSIPPI RIVER
ST PAUL
N
S
E
W

CEDARHURST MANSION COTTAGE GROVE

PRESCOTT LIFT BRIDGE

APPROX. TOTAL TOUR MILES 85

INTEREST POINT

FOOD

HISTORIC SITE

ANTIQUES

PARK

SCENIC ROUTE

MUSEUM

TOUR 14 KARL OSKAR AND SWEDISH SETTLERS

KARL AND KRISTINA STATUE

YESTERFARM OF MEMORIES

VALKOMMEN! Take your *flickas* and *poikas* (girls and boys) and head for a pleasant day. You will discover many lakes (24 in the tour area), museums, fine eating places, historic churches and memorabilia galore. You will soon realize that you are in "Little Sweden" where lutefisk, krumkake and egga doppa are familiar. Here live the descendents of immigrants who came from Sweden's worn-out soil to pioneer in a rich and stoneless Smaland. In July, the ethnic heritage is celebrated with Karl Oskar Days.

Who is Karl Oskar? He is a fictitious character in Vilhelm Moberg's four-book epic about immigrants. Karl Oskar Nilsson and his wife Kristina landed at Taylors Falls and went west a short distance to establish a claim. Land sold for $1.25 an acre. Many others came to populate the area, and it is said that even the Indians learned to speak Swedish. The immigrants hunted rabbits, squirrels, partridge, pheasants and deer, all of which were abundant. They farmed corn, wheat and flax. Take time to explore the roads around the lakes and stop at the interest points.

INTEREST POINTS

1. FOREST LAKE An interesting lakeside town with shops and restaurants.
2. CHISAGO CITY In the town square are a caboose (fun for picture taking) and cheese, gift and antique shops.
3. LINDSTROM The statue of Karl and Kristina Nilsson stands near the Dinner Bell Restaurant. A Swedish Coffee Shop and Swedish Bakery tempt visitors.
4. CENTER CITY The 1856 CHISAGO LAKES CHURCH is the oldest Lutheran church in Minnesota and has historic displays of Swedish origin, 612/257-6300, tours.
   THE HAZEL MAGNUSON MUSEUM and SUMMIT BOULEVARD with quaint houses, plus a vintage COURTHOUSE and COMMISSIONER'S ROW are places you will not want to miss in Center City.
5. YESTERFARM OF MEMORIES MUSEUM, 7 miles N of US 8 (take Co. Rd. 9/12 to Co. Rd. 20), Center City, 55012. 612/257-4234. The museum overflows with pioneer relics. May 1 to Nov. 1. Modest fee.
6. TAYLORS FALLS A truly beautiful area with picnic sites, boat cruises, bluffs to climb, pot-holes and unique rock formations. Visit the historic FULSOM HOUSE and the authentically preserved TAYLORS FALLS JAIL. Call 612/405-5245 for the TAYLORS FALLS QUEEN riverboat cruises.
7. 7 miles N on Co. Rd. 16 is the WILD MOUNTAIN ALPINE WATER SLIDE AREA. Various activities include wet and dry slides and picnic sites. Wild Mountain Recreation, Box 225, Taylors Falls, MN, 55084, Twin City toll-free 612/462-7550.
8. SCANDIA The GAMMELGARDEN MUSEUM is a replica of an immigrant settlement, 20880 Olinda Tr. N., Scandia, MN 55073, 612/433-5053.

Drive back to Forest Lake and reminisce about the pioneers who braved many hardships to settle this area.

RESTAURANTS ADJACENT TO ROUTE

A. FOREST LAKE A number of restaurants are available.
   Trout-Haus, 14536 W. Freeway Dr., a unique restaurant where you may catch your own meal all year-round, 612/464-2964.

B. TAYLORS FALLS The Chisago House, 311 Bench St., 612/465-5245.

C. LINDSTROM The Dinner Bell Restaurant, on Co. Rd. 8 in Lindstrom.
   Swedish Inn, 12960 Lake Blvd., 612/257-4072.

FOREST LAKE, CHISAGO CITY, LINDSTROM, CENTER CITY TAYLORS FALLS and SCANDIA

YESTERFARM OF MEMORIES

TAYLORS FALLS BEAUTY

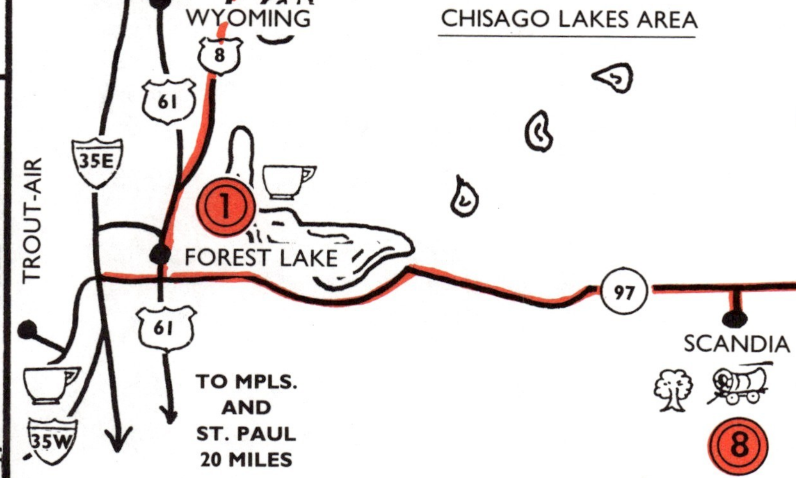

APPROX. TOTAL TOUR MILES 65 · INTEREST POINT · FOOD · HISTORIC SITE · ANTIQUES · PARK · SCENIC ROUTE · MUSEUM

TOUR 15 MINNEAPOLIS ARTS AND ANTIQUES

Art has many forms, and this tour provides an impression of several. Included area greeting card design, antique shops with varied specialities, stained glass windows, historical and European collections, an art institute and a building mural.

Minneapolis is rich in cultural assets, with many fine museums and art galleries and a wealth of antique dealers. A selection was made to give a variety of artistic experiences.

Follow this tour route to increase awareness of the beauty in historic treasures and unusual aspects of art. Contemporary and heritage examples are included. There are more interest points listed than needed for a one-day tour so you may choose those that appeal to you.

Depending on your personal desire to move along or to browse — you might do all or part of the tour in one day. You may find suggestions here to use as the basis for numerous tours.

Telephone numbers are given to allow checking ahead to determine what days and hours the attractions are open. A tour may be started at any point that is convenient for you. The MINNESOTA TRAVEL INFORMATION CENTER has an ARTS AND ATTRACTIONS GUIDE and a SPRING/SUMMER, FALL, or WINTER CALENDER OF EVENTS brochure available to further help you know what is going on in town.

Call or write the MINNESOTA TRAVEL INFORMATION CENTER, 240 Bremer Bldg., 419 Robert St., St. Paul, MN 55101. Minneapolis/St. Paul 612/296-5029, in Minnesota 800/652-9747, outside Minnesota 800/328-1461.

INTEREST POINTS

1. REINDEER HOUSE 3409 W. 44th St., 612/920-4741, greeting cards, tours.
2. ANTIQUE SHOPS at 50th St. and Xerxes.
3. LAKEWOOD MAUSOLEUM AND CHAPEL, 3600 Hennepin Av., stained glass windows, 612/822-2171, tours.
4. LAGOON ANTIQUES, Lake St. at Emerson, 50 dealers.
5. WALKER ART CENTER, Vineland Place, 612/375-7600, tours, Wed. 11 a.m., Sat and Sun. 2 p.m., group tours arranged, 612/375-7610.
6. SEVERAL ANTIQUE DEALERS 123 N. Washington, 121 N. Washington, 210 3rd Ave. N, 50 dealers.
7. MURAL BY PETER BUSA, VALSPAR CORP., 1101 S. 3rd St.
8. HENNEPIN COUNTY HISTORICAL SOCIETY 2303 3rd Ave. S., 612/870-1329, self-guided tour.
9. MINNEAPOLIS SOCIETY OF FINE ARTS, MINNEAPOLIS INSTITUTE OF ARTS, MINNEAPOLIS COLLEGE OF ART AND DESIGN 2400 3rd Ave. S., 612/874-0400, fee, tours.
10. AMERICAN SWEDISH INSTITUTE, Minnesota's Swedish heritage, 2600 Park Ave., 612/871-4907, fee, tours.
11. ANTIQUES, MINNESOTA 1516 E. Lake, 80 dealers, 612/722-6000.

FREDERICK R. WEISMAN ART MUSEUM
333 E. River Road, at the University of Minnesota.
Futuristic building, versatile art, FREE. Mon.-Fri. 10:00-6:00, Sat.-Sun. noon-5:00.

GALLERIES AND CENTERS THAT OFFER GROUP TOURS. Art Center of Minnesota, 2240 North Shore Drive, Orono, MN 612/473-7361. Raven Gallery, 3827 W. 50th St., African American Museum of Art and History, 2429 S. 8th St., 612/332-3506, group tours for young people. Lutheran Brotherhood Gallery, 625 4th Ave. S., 612/340-7000. Asian Fine Arts, 850 Baker Bldg., 612/333-4740. The Beard Art Galleries, Inc., 18th, 19th, and 20th century fine art, 1104 Nicollet, 612/332-5592. Cultural Exchange Co., 1608 Harmon Place. African, European, Asian, Mexican, Russian, Caribbean and Hispanic. 612/375-0065.

ART CENTERS AND MUSEUMS LISTED IN OTHER TOURS: Tour 2, University Art Museum, Tour 32: Edina Art Center; Tour 26, Bloomington Art Center.

TOUR 15 VERSATILITY OF ARTISTIC EXPERIENCES

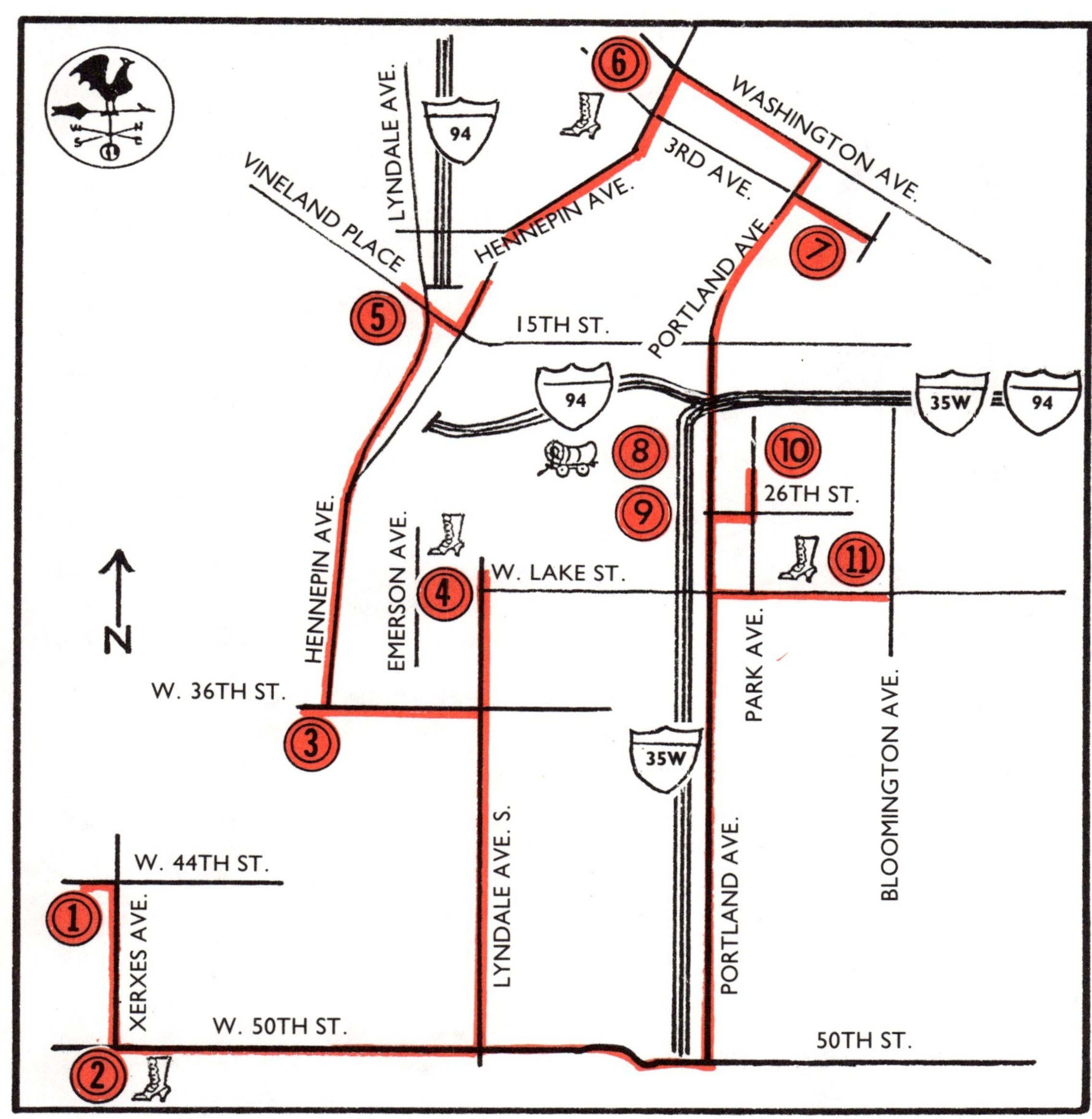

APPROX. TOTAL TOUR MILES

Tour Choice

INTEREST POINT

FOOD

HISTORIC SITE

ANTIQUES

PARK

SCENIC ROUTE ----

MUSEUM

TOUR 16 FOUR FAMOUS PERSONS TREK

This tour recognizes four famous persons. Charles Lindbergh, Jr. lived at Little Falls as a boy. He became famous when he flew non-stop from New York to Paris in 1927. His single engine monoplane was called the *Spirit of St. Louis*. Later in life he worked in scientific fields and was a speaker and a writer.

Anne Morrow Lindbergh was a skilled airplane pilot even before her marriage to Charles Lindbergh, Jr. She, too, became a well-known writer.

Sinclair Lewis wrote a scathing novel about small town life which he patterned after his home town. He later won both Pulitzer and Nobel prizes for novels that he wrote.

Dorothy Thompson Lewis was the second wife of Sinclair Lewis. She was a celebrated columnist and the first woman to head a foreign office for a major American newspaper. Her column, "On The Record," was syndicated in over 200 newspapers.

INTEREST POINTS

1. ST. CLOUD is located at the tip of navigation on the Mississippi. A former 1968 quarry is now the site of the Minnesota State Reformatory. The Stearns County Heritage Museum has multi-media presentations, 215 S. 33rd Ave., 612/253-8424. Locate the St. Cloud Area Chamber of Commerce at 20 S. 4th St., Box 487, St. Cloud, MN 56302, 320/251-2940.
2. LITTLE FALLS is the boyhood home of Charles A. Lindbergh. The Lindbergh Interpretive Center and home are open to the public and tours are available, Co. Rd. 52, May-Oct., 10-5 p.m., 612/632-9050, free. The Charles Weyerhauser Memorial Museum is also free. The Dewey-Radke Mansion in Pine Grove Park, Co. Rd. 27 W, 320/632-5775, is free, and the park has picnic grounds and a zoo.
3. FORT RIPLEY A side loop seven mi. N on MN 371 will bring you to Fort Ripley. Inquire at the main entrance gate for tour information and directions to the Military Interpretive Center. The fort is the largest US National Guard Training Camp in America with 53,000 acres, 320/632-4007.
4. 3 CHOICES Traveling W on MN 27 you have several choices of roads to reach Sauk Centre.
5. SAUK CENTRE This boyhood home of Sinclair Lewis has a Sinclair Lewis Interpretive Center at the junction of I-94 and US 71. The Sinclair Lewis home is at Sinclair Lewis Ave., open June-Sept., call 320/352-5201 for information on either.
6. BIRCH LAKE STATE FOREST is a quiet wooded area with a park that has picnic sites, beach and trails. From Melrose take Co. Rd. 13 N to Co. Rd. 17, go E 1 ½ mi., N 12 mi., then E on Forest Rd.
7. COLLEGEVILLE The 2400-acre campus of St. John's University and Abbey is an inspiring tour. Take home St. John's bread or have good food in the cafeteria, The Benedictines, Collegeville, MN 56321, 320/363-2011.
8. ST. JOSEPH Visit The College of St. Benedict, 320/363-5011.

RESTAURANTS ADJACENT TO ROUTE

A. Michael's Cafe, 262 Central Ave., Long Prairie, 320/732-2624.

B. Palmer House Restaurant, 1909, Sinclair Lewis Avenue and Main St., Sauk Centre, 320/352-3431.

C. Pine Edge Inn, 308 First St., S.E., Little Falls, 320/632-6681.

TOUR 16

ST. CLOUD, LITTLE FALLS, and SAUK CENTRE

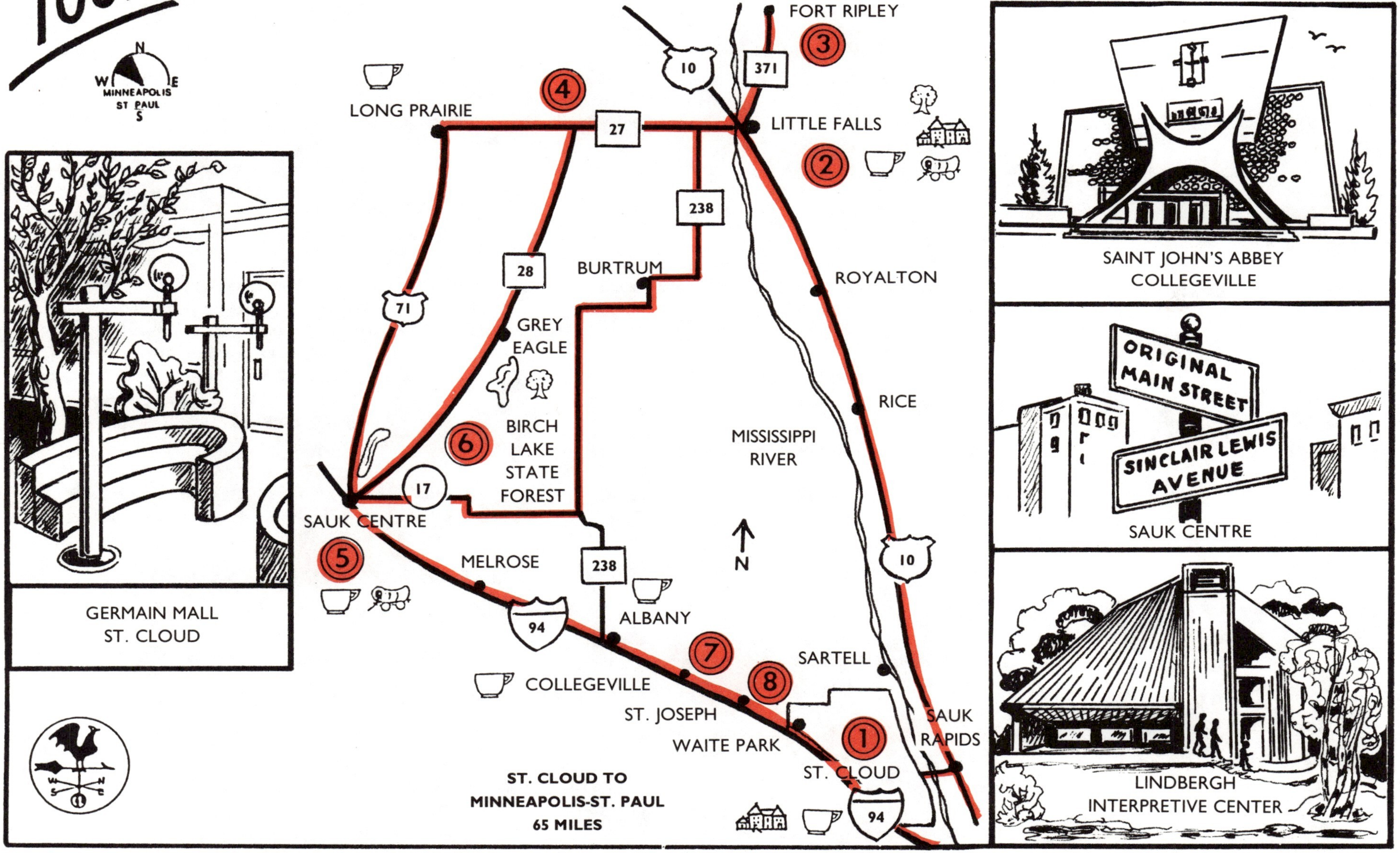

N
W E
MINNEAPOLIS
ST PAUL
S

FORT RIPLEY
3
10
371
4
LONG PRAIRIE
27
LITTLE FALLS
2
238
28
BURTRUM
ROYALTON
71
GREY
EAGLE
BIRCH
LAKE
STATE
FOREST
6
RICE
MISSISSIPPI
RIVER
17
SAUK CENTRE
N
10
5
MELROSE
238
94
ALBANY
7
SARTELL
8
COLLEGEVILLE
ST. JOSEPH
SAUK
RAPIDS
1
WAITE PARK
ST. CLOUD
94

ST. CLOUD TO
MINNEAPOLIS-ST. PAUL
65 MILES

SAINT JOHN'S ABBEY
COLLEGEVILLE

ORIGINAL
MAIN STREET
SINCLAIR LEWIS
AVENUE
SAUK CENTRE

LINDBERGH
INTERPRETIVE CENTER

GERMAIN MALL
ST. CLOUD

INTEREST POINT

SCENIC ROUTE - - - -

TOUR 17 HAPPY HOOTENANNY A JOYOUS DAY

SEPPMAN MILL
MINNEOPA STATE PARK

OTTAWA METHODIST CHURCH
ST. PETER

Follow the Minnesota River through countryside and rolling prairie. Rich in heritage, these towns have preserved their origins in museums and restorations. Head south on US 169 and make your first stop at Jordan. Take time to walk the Main Street where you will find an antique store, an old-time meat market and small town flavor. You will have begun a pleasant day that all ages can enjoy. The tour roams through Belle Plaine where a surprise awaits you, to Le Sueur, home of the Jolly Green Giant, to Ottawa, St. Peter and Mankato.

You will pass rich land, natural beauty and remnants of great woods as you follow the trail that pioneers and settlers etched. Each community has interesting sights to offer. Relax and leave the highways as you explore and discover.

INTEREST POINTS

1. JORDAN Gramma's Attic & Old Time Store, 208-214 Water St., 612/492-2566. Also old-time shops for meats, food and bakery goods.
2. BELLE PLAINE At harvest time this is a fun stop to see the unusual Halloween displays at Emma Krumbee's Restaurant and Apple Shop. What is the surprise? Drive into Belle Plaine on MN 25 or Meridian (just south of Krumbee's), and turn right on Court. The Hooper-Hillstrom House is here. Yes, here's the world's eighth wonder — a two-story, six-seater outhouse! Hope you have your camera along.
3. LE SUEUR W. W. Mayo House, the home of William Morrell Mayo where he lived previous to establishing the world-renowned Mayo Clinic in Rochester.
4. OTTAWA N of St. Peter are the Township Hall and the Ottawa Methodist Church, built in 1858, and now the Le Sueur County Museum.
5. TRAVERSE DES SIOUX One mile NW of St. Peter is the site of an 1858 treaty signing with the Sioux, picnic sites and trails.
6. ST. PETER The E. St. Julien Cox House was once the social hub of the area. Gustavus Adolphus College with its famous Christ Chapel and Nobel Hall is an exciting tour. The Episcopal Church of the Holy Communion at 118 N. Minnesota is rich in tradition. The St. Peter State Hospital has an impressive new facility in addition to an 1880 Museum. Both are located at the south end of town. The St. Peter Woolen Mill dates back to 1867. All have tours available, and the St. Peter Area Chamber of Commerce has further information, St. Peter, MN 56082. Note location on the detail map. For Gustavus Adolphus College, call 507/931-7676.
7. MANKATO A wide choice of activity and sightseeing await in Mankato. The Hubbard House Museum has Indian and pioneer history. Mankato State University, Bethany College and the Sisters of Notre Dame Convent (with Craft Shop and Chapel) all are located here. A Carnival, Festival and the Mahkato Mdewakanton Pow Wow are events you would enjoy. "Betsy-Tacy" storybooks originated here. Minneopa State Park, with the old stone Seppman Mill and lovely Minneopa Falls is located 6 mi. W of Mankato. Contact the Blue Earth County Museum located in the 1871 historic Hubbard House at 604 Broad St., Mankato, MN 56001, 507/345-4154.

RESTAURANTS ADJACENT TO ROUTE

A. Belleview Restaurant, US 169 N., Belle Plaine, 612/873-6577.
B. Emma Krumbees Restaurant, US 169, Belle Plaine, 612/445-1000.
C. Coachlight Inn, US 169 and MN 93, Le Sueur, 507/665-3351.
D. Holiday House, MN 22 S., St. Peter, 507/931-3910.
E. Prairie House Family Restaurant, 605 S. Minnesota, St. Peter, 507/931-6464.
F. Copper Alley, 1655 Mankato Mall, Mankato, 507/625-2316.

TOUR 17 BELLE PLAINE, ST. PETER and MANKATO

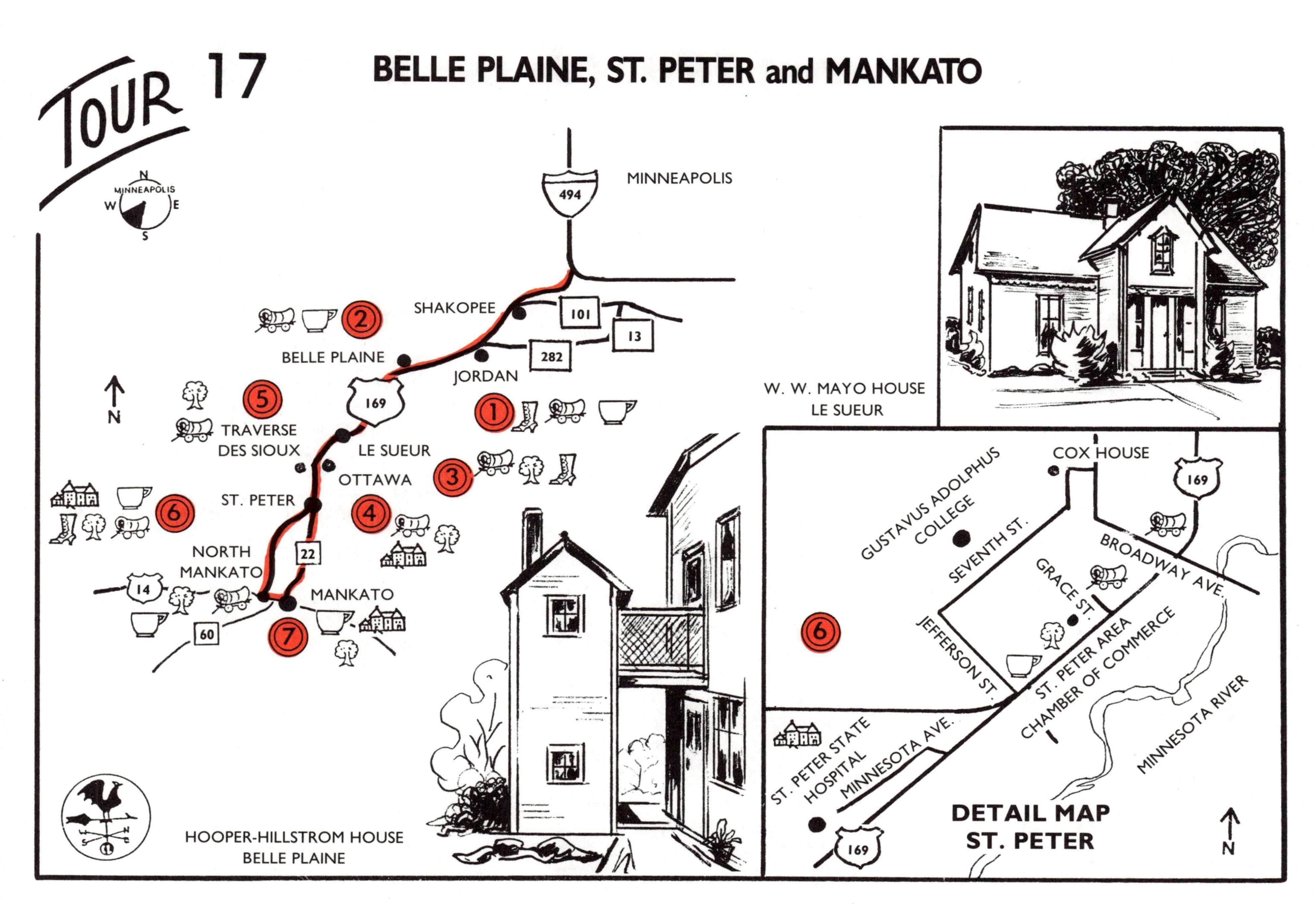

APPROX. TOTAL TOUR MILES 160   INTEREST POINT   FOOD   HISTORIC SITE   ANTIQUES   PARK   SCENIC ROUTE   MUSEUM

TOUR 18 MINNEAPOLIS, CITY OF LAKES

LAKE HARRIET STREETCAR

WATERBIRDS
THRIVE ON THE LAKES

Minneapolis offers an invitation to a beautiful tour route of lakes and leisure on parkways all worthy of a scenic designation. This unusual asset is lovely in any season. There are, unbelievably, 22 lakes, 153 parks and 55 miles of paved pathways, all within the city limits. Enjoy biking, jogging, walking, and roller skating.

The major chain-of-lakes embraces Cedar Lake, Lake-of-the-Isles, Lake Calhoun, Lake Harriet and Lake Nokomis, plus many other lakes throughout the city. Fishing and boating are popular pastimes and picnic sites and playgrounds are plentiful. Canoes, sailboats, windsurfers and kayaks float like bright moths on blue waters in the summer. In winter cross-country and downhill skiing, sledding and tubing, ice skating, ice sailing and ice fishing change the scene against a snowy backdrop.

The name Minneapolis means a "city of water" (a Dakota-Greek conjunction). Get out of your car at each interest point to explore the distinct character of these individual settings.

INTEREST POINTS

1. LAKE HIAWATHA Golf course, playground and beach, 27th Ave. S. and E. 44th St., 612/348-8326.
2. LAKE NOKOMIS PARK 200 acres, trails, swimming, fishing, sailboating and canoeing, 2401 E. Minnehaha Parkway, 612/348-8027.
3. DIAMOND LAKE and PEARL PARK Playgrounds and sports fields, 414 E. Diamond Lake Rd., 612/348-5765.
4. LAKE HARRIET and PARK with 400 acres have many attractions. COMO-HARRIET STREETCAR, runs between Lake Harriet and Lake Calhoun (1908, OLD 1300), modest fee, 42nd St. and Lake Harriet Blvd., 612/348-2243/522-7417.
   LAKE HARRIET BANDSHELL Concerts and performances, N side of Lake Harriet at William Berry Pkwy., 612/348-2121/348-2226. LYNDALE PARK GARDENS include rock garden and fountains, Lake Harriet Pkwy. at Roseway Road. LAKE HARRIET QUEEN-OF-LAKES sternwheeler, 3 lakes, modest fee, May 31-Labor Day, 612/729-8142. THOMAS SADLER ROBERTS BIRD SANCTUARY 13 acres on Lake Harriet Pkwy. near the bandshell. It is named for the "Father of Ornithology," with 200 species of birds seen here (two-thirds of the species found in Minnesota), 612/348-2226.
5. LAKE CALHOUN PARK A ship's bell and mast accent this 524-acre park, canoe and fishing boat rentals, walking and jogging paths, sailing and fishing, Lake Calhoun Pkwy. at W. Lake St., 612/729-8142.
6. LAKE OF THE ISLES Two islands on this lake have wildlife sanctuaries and bird nesting grounds, as well as biking, walking, and jogging paths.
7. CEDAR LAKE has total lake and park area of 252 acres, with jogging, walking and biking trails, 612/348-2243.
8. THEODORE WIRTH PARK is the largest of the parks and has summer activities plus outstanding winter sports that include downhill and cross-country skiing, ski jumping, ice skating, ice fishing, ice sailing, sledding and tubing. ELOISE BUTLER WILDFLOWER GARDEN AND BIRD SANCTUARY is located here, naturalist guided tours, entrance 1/2 mi. N of US 12 on Theodore Wirth Pkwy., 612/348-5702.
9. LORING PARK has a small jewel lake located in the city's heart, at 15th and Willow Sts., 612/348-8226.
10. POWDERHORN PARK has a lake in a deep amphitheater setting, E. 34th St. and 15th Ave. S., 612/348-4512.

At Lake Street and Hennepin Avenue in Calhoun Square are specialty shops and restaurants. A step-on guide will escort groups in a tour of lovely old homes and historic points. Book ahead 612/335-1760, no fee. Buses may need a permit to drive on the parkways, call 612/348-2226.

RESTAURANTS ADJACENT TO ROUTE

Restaurants abound in these areas.

A. Calhoun Square, W. Lake Street at Hennepin Avenue.

B. Hennepin Avenue from Lake St. to Loring Park.

TOUR 18 CHAIN OF LAKES, POWDERHORN, DIAMOND and LORING LAKES

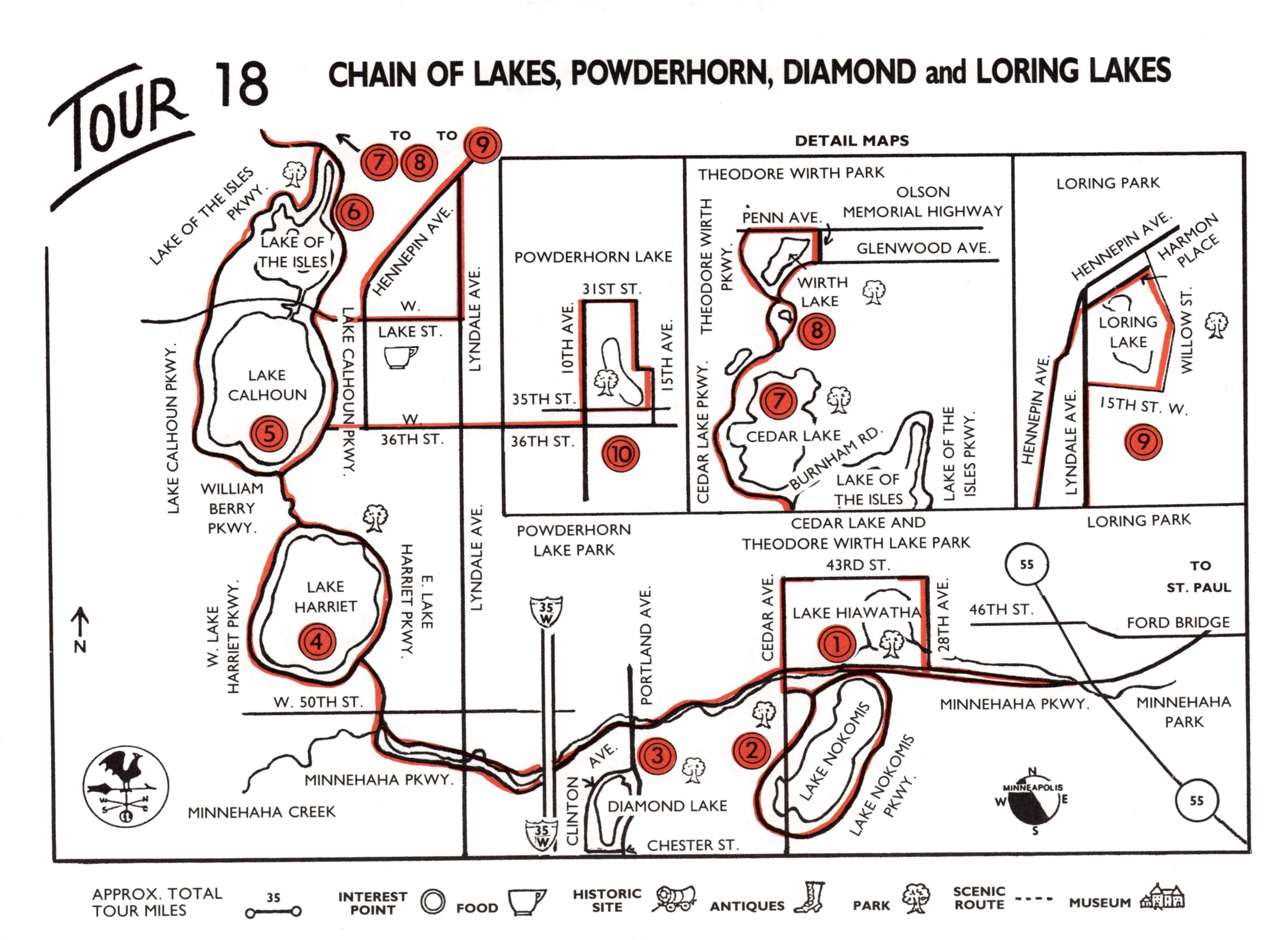

TOUR 19 A TRAGIC FIRE AND LAKELAND LORE

N
W E
S
MINNEAPOLIS
ST PAUL

This colorful tour is rich in history. A major highlight is at Hinckley where the story is told of a devastating fire that ravaged 400 square miles, wiped out 6 towns and took 418 lives. A heroic train engineer saved many lives and this story is told by survivors who recorded this tragic event. The Mission Creek Theme Park has a train ride, animals, shops and continuous events.

You will enjoy following the shoreline of Mille Lacs Lake. The Mille Lacs Lake Indian Museum is a rewarding stop. Brainerd is a relaxing area with a 50-foot Paul Bunyan, an amusement park, helicopter rides and many fun choices. You will find Lumbertown, U.S.A. offers history and dining lumberjack style. Most of the attractions are open from Memorial Day weekend to Labor Day. Take your time and enjoy this special tour.

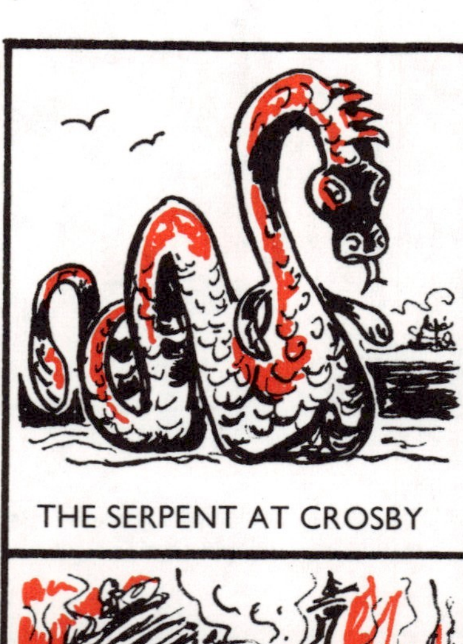

THE SERPENT AT CROSBY

THE GREAT FIRE OF 1894

INTEREST POINTS

1. NORTHWEST COMPANY FUR POST 1 ½ mi. W of Pine City on Co. Rd. 7, 612/629-6356, history of fur trading, an 1804 restoration.
2. HINCKLEY FIRE MUSEUM I-35 Interchange, history of 1894 disaster, Hinckley State Monument, 32-mile fire trail. Mission Creek Theme Park, 1894 atmosphere and events, 320/384-7600.
3. PINE COUNTY MUSEUM Askov.
4. MILLE LACS LAKE (Indian name "Spirit Lake") 18 mi. long, 14 mi. wide, Father Hennepin Memorial. Follow route to Aitkin.
5. At Crosby visit the CUYUNA RANGE HISTORICAL MUSEUM.
6. BRAINERD PAUL BUNYAN AMUSEMENT CENTER, MN 210 and 371, 218/829-6242, CROW WING COUNTY MUSEUM in Court House, LUMBERTOWN, U.S.A., 218/829-2811. A fun area with much to explore.
7. GARRISON Capital of Walleye Lakes, the Gold Coast, City Hall Museum, fishing resorts, Forest Lookout Tower, Ak-Sar-Ben Gardens.
8. MILLE LACS INDIAN RESERVATION AND MUSEUM.
9. MILLE LACS LAKE KATHIO STATE PARK and Interpretive Center.
10. MILACA VILLAGE HALL MUSEUM.
11. SHERBURNE NATIONAL WILDLIFE REFUGE.

RESTAURANTS ADJACENT TO ROUTE

A. Red Shed, on I-35, Pine City, 612/629-3416.
B. Alpine City Inn, I-35 and Co. Rd. 324, Pine City, 612/629-6665.
C. Cassidy's, I-35, Hinckley, 320/384-6129.
D. Hardee's, 401 Fire Monument Rd. Hinckley, 320/384-6098.
E. Tobies Restaurant, I-35 and MN 49, Hinckley, 320/384-6174.
F. Banning Junction, 2812 MN 23, Finlayson, 320/245-9989.
G. Bar Harbor Supper Club, 6512 Interlachen Rd., Brainerd, 218/963-2568.
H. The Chinese Phoenix Restaurant, MN 371 N., Brainerd, 218/963-4658.
I. Hasse, MN 210 E., Brainerd, 218/829-1441.
J. Holiday Inn, MN 371 So., Brainerd, 218/829-1441
K. Iven's on the Bay, MN 371 So., Brainerd, 218/829-9872.
L. Kavanaugh's, 2300 Kavanaugh Dr., Brainerd, 218/829-5226.
M. Sawmill Inn, MN 210 and 371, Brainerd, 218/829-5444.
N. Westside Cafe, 801 W. Washington, Brainerd, 218/829-5561.
O. Granny's Kitchen, Fort Mille Lacs Village, Onamia, 320/532-3651.
P. K-Bob Cafe, 109 LaGrande Ave. S., Princeton, 612/389-1361.

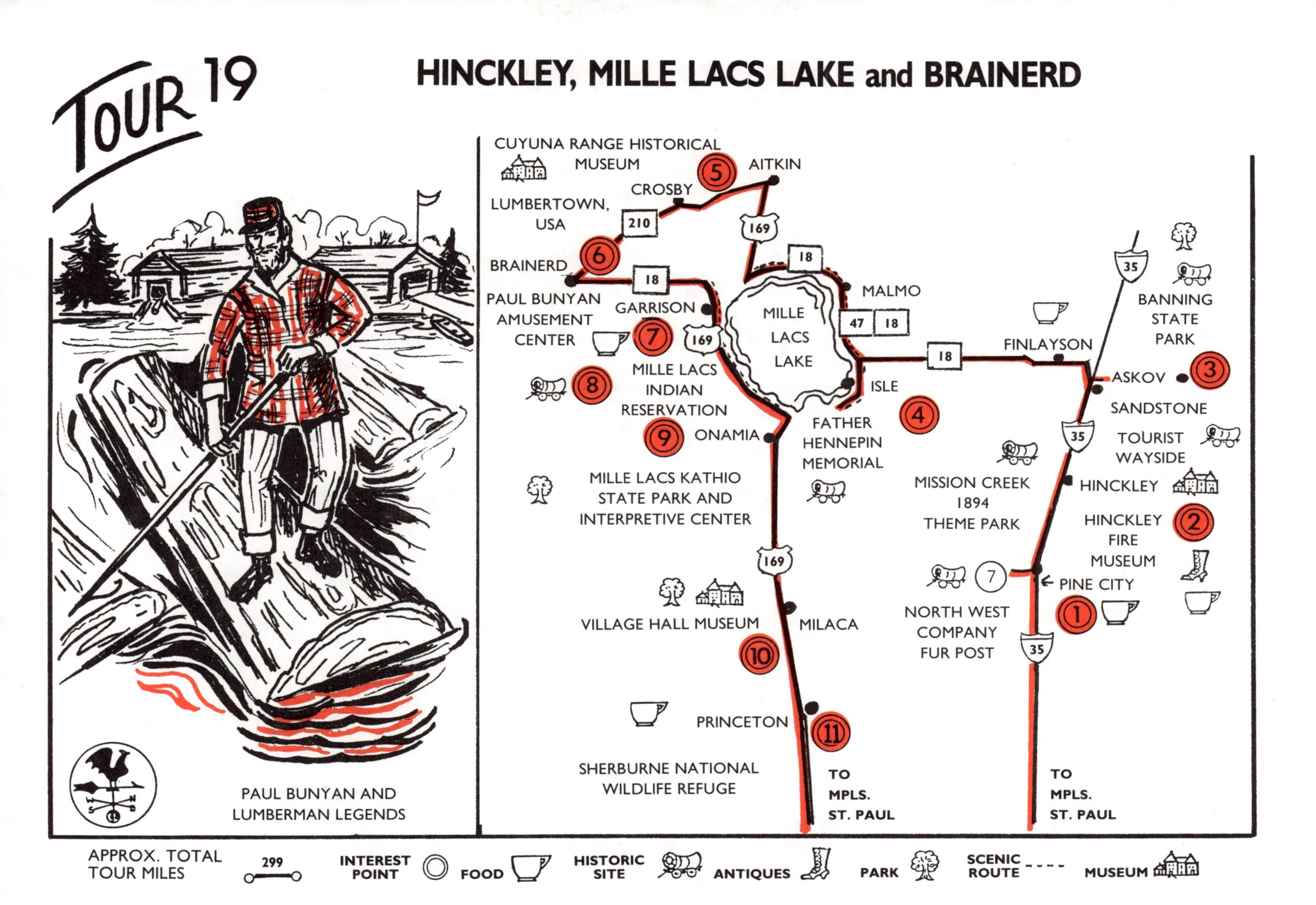
TOUR 19
HINCKLEY, MILLE LACS LAKE and BRAINERD
CUYUNA RANGE HISTORICAL MUSEUM
5
AITKIN
CROSBY
LUMBERTOWN, USA
210
169
6
BRAINERD
18
PAUL BUNYAN AMUSEMENT CENTER
GARRISON
7
169
MILLE LACS LAKE
MALMO
47
18
18
FINLAYSON
35
BANNING STATE PARK
8
MILLE LACS INDIAN RESERVATION
ISLE
ASKOV
3
SANDSTONE
4
9
ONAMIA
FATHER HENNEPIN MEMORIAL
35
TOURIST WAYSIDE
MILLE LACS KATHIO STATE PARK AND INTERPRETIVE CENTER
MISSION CREEK 1894 THEME PARK
HINCKLEY
HINCKLEY FIRE MUSEUM
2
169
7
PINE CITY
NORTH WEST COMPANY FUR POST
1
VILLAGE HALL MUSEUM
MILACA
10
35
PRINCETON
11
SHERBURNE NATIONAL WILDLIFE REFUGE
TO MPLS. ST. PAUL
TO MPLS. ST. PAUL
PAUL BUNYAN AND LUMBERMAN LEGENDS
APPROX. TOTAL TOUR MILES
299
INTEREST POINT
FOOD
HISTORIC SITE
ANTIQUES
PARK
SCENIC ROUTE
MUSEUM

TOUR 20 COUNTRYSIDE AND LITTLE MOUNTAIN

COUNTRY BEAUTY

OLIVER H. KELLEY HOMESTEAD
ELK RIVER

This relaxing tour follows open, rolling country side roads rather than freeways. There is much to discover on slower-paced byways. At Monticello you will find a promontory that rises above the flat prairies. Lakes dot the plains below and shimmer in the sunlight. Two power plants can be seen in the distance on the Mississippi River.

Two riverside parks welcome you to picnic where the bridge crosses the Mississippi.

Step into the past at Jamison's LITTLE MOUNTAIN SETTLEMENT MUSEUM where log homes are furnished with Norwegian and Swedish artifacts of the 1870 period.

Lake Maria, 8 miles west of Monticello, has a remainder of the hardwood forest that once covered this area. An interpretive center tells of hawks, loons, great blue herons and other birds as well as marshes, lakes and terminal moraine ridges found in the park.

A tour of the Sherco Power Plant includes films and a greenhouse and is one you won't want to miss.

The Oliver Hudson Kelley Homestead near Elk River is a living history farm with related activities. Oliver H. Kelley was founder of the National Grange (the Patrons of Husbandry), and this home built in 1869 served as the first headquarters of the national farm organization. Elk River derives its name from the huge herds of elk that once inhabited this vicinity. There are picnic sites along the Mississippi River in Elk River. Highway US 10 or I-94 will return you to the Twin Cities.

INTEREST POINTS

1. Turn off I-94 at Dayton or Fletcher and drive W to St. Michael through PEACEFUL RURAL ROADS. In Albertville note the old church and its cemetery.
2. MONTICELLO Turn S on Co. Rd. 117 and drive to Little Mountain to enjoy the view. Return to I-94 and take Territorial Road to LITTLE MOUNTAIN SETTLEMENT MUSEUM, Box 581 Monticello, MN 55362, 612/295-1950. Open Sat. and Sun. 1-5 p.m., May-Oct. Group Tours. Special Celebration Days, Antique and Book Shop.
3. LAKE MARIA STATE PARK Take Co. Rd. 39 to the Interpretive Center at the park, trails, picnic sites, boat and canoe rental, 612/878-2325.
4. SHERCO POWER PLANT Follow map to Clearwater, cross the bridge to Clear Lake and turn E to Becker. Co. Rd. 8 will take you to the plant. Check in at the guard house. Arrange a tour by calling 612/330-5506.
5. SHERBURNE NATIONAL WILDLIFE REFUGE and SAND DUNES STATE FOREST This is an interesting park with varied trails, an Indian village, many birds and view sites. The Dunes are planted to trees. Co. Rd. 9 at Zimmerman, 612/389-3323.
6. OLIVER H. KELLEY FARM Mid-19th century agricultural activities are demonstrated, open May-October, 10-5 p.m. daily, modest fee, 15788 Kelley Farm Rd , Elk River, MN, 612/441-6896.

RESTAURANTS ADJACENT TO ROUTE

A. River Inn, Monticello, 612/263-2409.

B. Stella's Cafe, 144 W. Broadway, Monticello, 612/295-9975.

C. Riverview, The Chalet, 10990 95th St. N.E., Monticello, 612/441-6833.

D. Monti Club, Co. Rd. 117, Monticello, 612/295-2211.

E. Prairie House Family Restaurant, US 169 N., Elk River, 612/441-7803.

F. Sneaky Pete's, 17323 US 10, Elk River, 612/441-2777.

G. Sunshine Depot, 701 Main St., Elk River, 612/441-1371.

H. Centennial Travel Plaza, I-94 and MN 24, Clearwater, 612/878-2613.

I. Prairie House Family Restaurant, I-94 and Clearlake Rd., Clearwater, 612/558-6326.

MONTICELLO, BIG LAKE and ELK RIVER

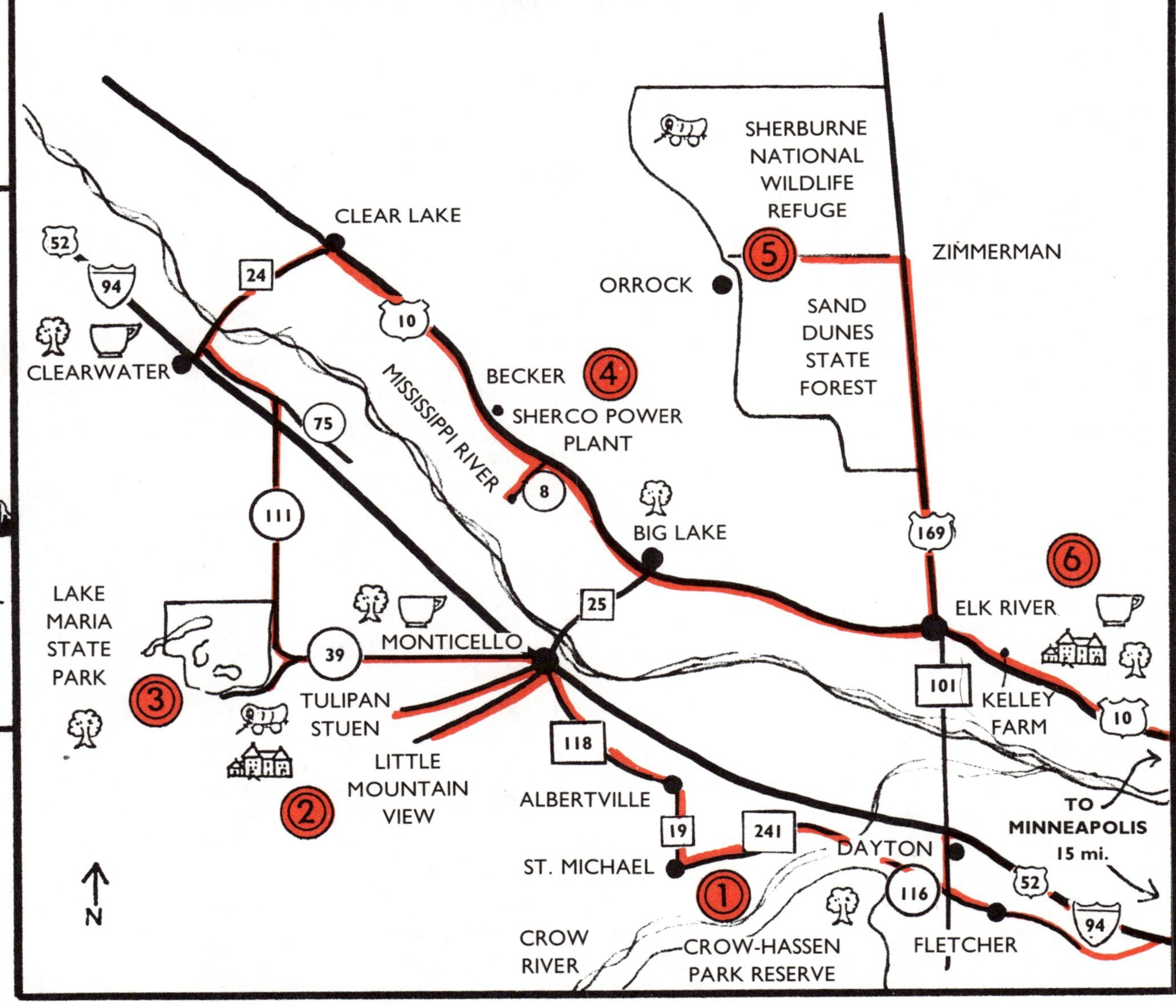

TULIPAN STUEN
LITTLE MOUNTAIN SETTLEMENT

APPROX. TOTAL TOUR MILES  

TOUR 21 VALLEY VENTURE FOR ENTERTAINMENT

JORDAN'S WATER STREET

APPLE ORCHARDS

MURPHY'S LANDING

There's adventure in the Minnesota Valley with entertainment galore and it's all just 25 minutes away from the Twin Cities. From I-494 take US 169 to MN 101 to begin a day of fun. Within a 15-mile radius are riverboat rides, an amusement park, horse racing, car racing, a 16th century festival, an 1840-1890 pioneer village, an apple orchard, and "Oldtown" mainstreet and a wealth of playland activities.

INTEREST POINTS

1. RACEWAY PARK For the stock race car enthusiast, 6528 MN 101, Shakopee, 612/445-2257.
2. VALLEY FAIR Minnesota's major amusement center covers 55 acres and includes an IMAX theatre six-stories high with an 82-foot-wide screen, water slides, 1920 carrousel, trolley, food, merchandise and games. 3 mi. E of Shakopee on MN 101, open mid-May-August, weekends in September, 612/445-6500.
3. MURPHY'S LANDING Minnesota Valley Restoration features a typical pioneer 1840-1890 village, German immigrant area, fur trader's home (Oliver Faribault), Dakota village, one-room brick school house, two settler's farmsteads, town square with church, general store and railroad depot. Tours on weekends or by appointment, open Tues.-Sat. in the summer and some winter days, 2187 MN 101, Shakopee, 612/ 445-6900.
4. CREATIVE RIVER TOURS Riverboat rides on the *Emma Lee* narrated with local history. Charters or public rides May-Oct., Wed.-Fri. 2-3 p.m., Sat.-Sun. 1-2, 3-4 p.m. For rates, reservations call 612/445-7491. The departure ramp is at Murphy's Landing.
5. MINNESOTA VALLEY GARDEN CENTER Seasonal garden and yard beautification; trees, flowers and decor. Browse among rows of bloom and green glory. 3232 W. 150th. St., Shakopee 612/445-9160.
6. MINNESOTA VALLEY MALL just S of Shakopee (1½ mi.) on US 169 you will find stores and restaurants.
7. MINNESOTA RENAISSANCE FESTIVAL A 16th century village is recreated in late August and early September with crafts, entertainment, musicians and villagers in authentic costumes, horse racing and jousts. A fall European harvest atmosphere features games and robust foods. Call 612/445-7361 for dates and information, 4 mi. S of Shakopee on US 169.
8. JORDAN This small town offers much fun and pleasure. A stroll down Water Street brings you to the Old City Hall of 1885, a settler's log cabin, Grandma's Antiques, Pekaran's oldtime meats, a bakery, and brewery ruins. Call Gail Anderson of Grandma's Attic Antiques (612/492-2566) and she'll tell you anything you want to know about the town (she is a former mayor).
9. SPONSEL'S MINNESOTA HARVEST APPLE ORCHARD Many varieties of apples are shown on a hayride tour and offered in mouth-watering baked goods. Open 7 days a week, S of Jordan on Old US 169 (Co. Rd. 61). Watch for signs to direct you up the hill, 612/492-2785. You'll find yourself on Apple Lover's Lane.

MINNESOTA VALLEY HIKING TRAIL extends from Ft. Snelling to LeSueur and has an access E of US 169 On MN 41. For information about this trail, city parks, or public swimming pool, call 612/445-2742.

RESTAURANTS ADJACENT TO ROUTE

SHAKOPEE

A. Happy Chef Restaurant, MN 101 E., 612/445-5659.

B. Perkins Family Restaurant, 1205 E. 1st Ave., 612/445-6475.

C. Dangerfield's, 1583 E. 1st Ave., Shakopee, 612/445-2245.

D. Wampach's Restaurant, 126 W. 1st Ave., 612/445-2721.

TOUR 21

MINNESOTA VALLEY'S ATTRACTIONS BECKON

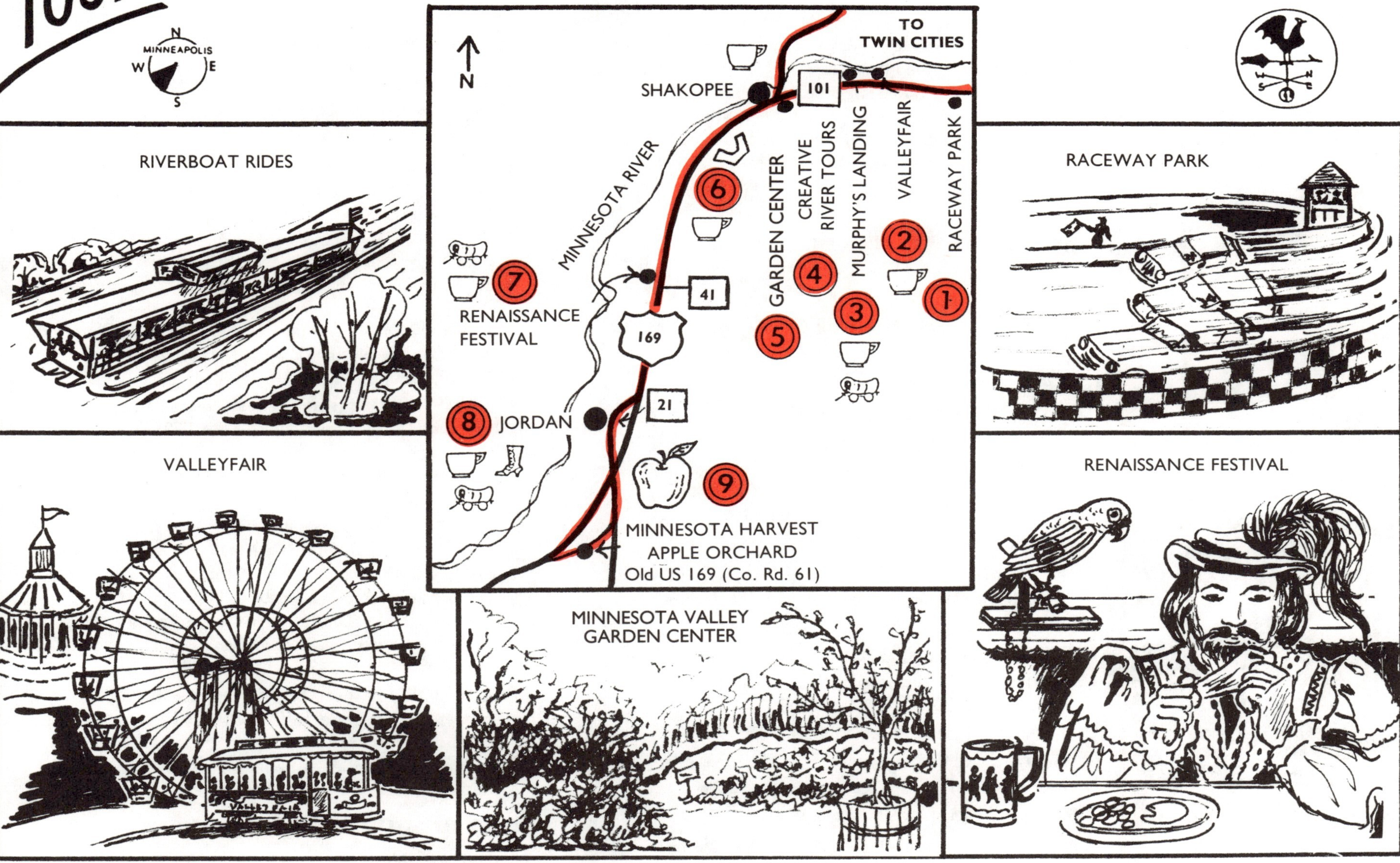

APPROX. TOTAL TOUR MILES  72

INTEREST POINT  FOOD  HISTORIC SITE  ANTIQUES  PARK  SCENIC ROUTE - - - - MUSEUM 

TOUR 22 CITY AND COUNTRY PLEASURES

SILVER LAKE

MAYO BROTHERS MEMORIAL

This tour introduces you to Rochester. Have you been to Silver Lake and Mayo Park, explored the Pedestrian Subway System or visited the Mayo Brothers Memorial? After you have become acquainted with the city, there is a beautiful bluff country south of the city that is delightful to drive through. Quaint towns are set in rugged rock outcropping backgrounds, with deep gorges and rippling streams and even mysterious caverns along the tour route. This combination of city and country vistas of beauty will be long remembered.

ROCHESTER WALKING OR DRIVING TOUR INTEREST POINTS

(See Circle Map)

1. Rochester Area Chamber of Commerce, 507/288-1122.
2. Rochester City Hall, attractive art deco style.
3. Bus Depot, 1899, historic brick building.
4. Mayo Park, peaceful walking area.
5. Mayo Civic Auditorium, varied events, 507/288-8475.
6. Rochester Civic Theatre, 507/282-7633.
7. Rochester Art Center, exhibits, 507/282-7633.
8. Rochester Public Library,, exhibits, 507/285-8000.
9. Wild Wings Art Gallery.
10. Heritage House, 1875, historic home, 507/288-6767.
11. Rochester Methodist Hospital, 507/286-7168.
12. Callaway Gardens.
13. Peacock Alley, in the Kahler Hotel lobby.
14. Mayo Medical Museum, human body studies, 507/284-3280.
15. Plummer Building, Carillon Bells, 1928.
16. Mayo Clinic Building, tours, 507/284-2653.
17. Guggenheim Building, contemporary design.
18. Hilton Building, modern design.
19. Calvary Episcopal Church, 1862, stained glass.

ON ROCHESTER'S PERIMETER ARE:

MAYOWOOD and the OLMSTED COUNTY HISTORICAL CENTER Mayowood is on the National Register of Historic Places, Co. Rd. 122 and Salem Rd. S.W., 507/282-9447.

COUNTRY DRIVE INTEREST POINTS

1. STEWARTVILLE US 63, Lake Florence Park.
2. SPRING VALLEY Lake Louise State Park, Methodist Church Museum, Pioneer Home Museum and ornate downtown 1855 buildings, Chamber of Commerce, Spring Valley, MN 55975.
3. PRESTON "The Trout Capital of Minnesota," historic Jail House Inn where guests sleep "behind bars," Preston Apple Farm, US 52 and MN 16, 507/765-4486, Filmore County Museum, and Forestville State Park with trails, horseback riding, and tours of the three interconnected caverns in the Mystery Caves (47 degrees all year), Co. Rd. 12, 507/352-5111.
4. HARMONY Minnesota's largest Amish Colony is here and offers handmade wares and tours, 507/886-2303/886-5392. You will find antiques, crafts and art at the Shamrock Mini Mall. Norseland Kitchens feature lefse and other Norwegian specialties, 507/864-2323. Niagara Cave has awe-inspiring stalactites, a crystal wedding chapel and a wishing well, Harmony, MN 55939, 507/886-6606.
5. LANESBORO Root River bluffs and quaint turn-of-the-century architecture, Lanesboro Historical Museum, State Trout Hatchery, Southeastern Minnesota Forest Reserve Resource Center. Contact Lanesboro Community Club, Lanesboro, MN 55949, 507/467-3722.
6. RUSHFORD claims to be "Turkey Hunting Capital" of Minnesota. The Ernie Tuff Museum and Tew's Mill, 1875, are located on the Root River as are lovely picnic sites. Contact Rushford Area Business Association, Box 3385, Rushford, MN 55971, 507/864-2444.

RESTAURANTS ADJACENT TO ROUTE

A copy of *The Visitor*, available at the Rochester Chamber of Commerce, or many locations, offers a choice of restaurants.

TOUR 22

ROCHESTER, and LOVELY BLUFF AREA TOWNS

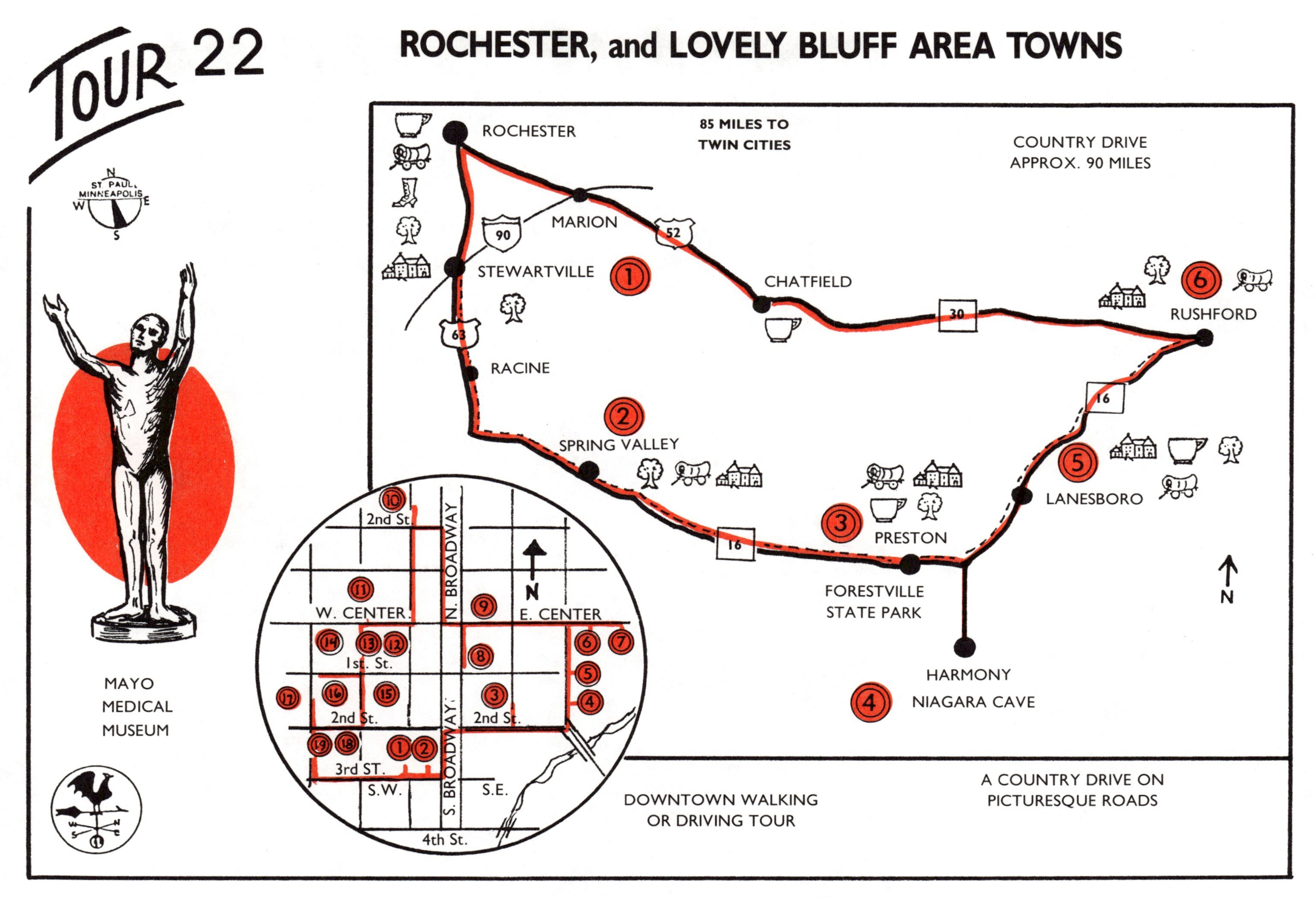

APPROX. TOTAL TOUR MILES 260

PARK SCENIC ROUTE MUSEUM

TOUR 23 ANNANDALE ADVENTURE

LAKE COUNTRY
100 LAKES IN 25 MILES

ANTIQUES,
A MUSEUM,
A PIONEER VILLAGE
AND COUNTY PARKS

This tour is a delightful break-a-way from daily routine. Where else but in Minnesota can you find 100 lakes within a 25-mile area? You will discover beautiful parks with beaches, picnic grounds, camping, fishing and trails. On this route, you will find antiques, lakeside roads, a museum, a restored hotel, the former home of Hubert H. Humphrey, an excellent pioneer village reproduction, lovely historic homes and lakes, lakes, lakes and more lakes.

INTEREST POINTS

1. MORRIS T. BAKER PARK Just S of town at Loretto, on Co. Rd. 19, you can circle part of the park on Co. Rds. 19, 24 and 201.
2. ROCKFORD The LAKE REBECCA PARK RESERVE is located S of MN 55 on Co. Rd. 50, 612/757-4700. At Rockford is the AMES-FLORIDA HOUSE, 8131 Bridge Rd., a Greek revival style home built during the period when Rockford boomed as it became the site of grist, lumber and woolen mills.
3. WALDON WOODS ANTIQUES is located between Rockford and Buffalo. For hours call 612/475-3031.
4. BUFFALO was not named for the animal, but for the buffalo fish. LAKE PULASKI, just N of town, for a pretty drive, follow Co. Rd. 3 on the east shore of the lake.
5. CAMP COURAGE and CAMP FRIENDSHIP have signs to show their location between Maple Lake and Annandale. Drive in to see these well-known camps. Also in this same location is MINNESOTA PIONEER PARK, a newly developed 23-building village that includes a repair shop, schoolroom, sod house, log cabin, church, animal petting farm and seasonal activities. Admission. 320/274-8489.
6. ANNANDALE is set in a chain-of-lakes. The recently restored THAYER HOTEL, built in 1895, is painted in elegant light blue with white balconies, 320/274-3371.
7. SCENIC ROAD Just beyond Annandale on MN 55 turn S on Co. Rd. 3. This country road leads past KOINONIA RETREAT, log buildings and rolling countryside.
8. COKATO The COKATO HISTORICAL MUSEUM has excellent exhibits relating to the area. A few miles E on US 12 is the DUSTIN MASSACRE HISTORICAL MARKER. Take time to read this information.
9. WAVERLY Once HUBERT HUMPHREY made this his home. Drive N on Co. Rd. 9, following the Lake Waverly shoreline to the N end of the lake where a white picket fence sets off the former property of the Humphreys. It is now a rehabilitation center.
10. HUMPHREY-ARENDT PARK is N of the Humphrey home on Co. Rd. 9. A memorial is erected here. Stand in this quiet spot where only a crow's call or a mourning dove's crooning break the silence. Walk to the bridge over the river for a sense of peace.
11. MAPLE PLAIN Continue on US 12 to Maple Plain. An unusual event occurs here during summer months. Polo matches are held at the WEST END FARM on weekends. Go S on Co. Rd. 90 and turn right at Turner Road. Take a picnic lunch and watch this fascinating game where fine horses are in action. A modest fee admits a carload to the clubhouse and grounds. Call 612/479-4307 for game schedules.

US 12 will return you to I-494. There are may be too many interest points to explore in one day; you choose the most appealing.

RESTAURANTS ADJACENT TO ROUTE

A. Gasthof Zur Gemuttlichkeit, W. US 12, Montrose, 612/675-3777.

B. Red's Pizza Family Restaurant, E. US 12, Howard Lake, 320/543-3331.

C. Thayer Hotel, MN 55 (downtown) Annandale, 320/274-3371.

D. Prairie House Family Restaurant, MN 55 E., Buffalo, 612/682-1226.

TOUR 23

BUFFALO, COKATO, ANNANDALE and WAVERLY

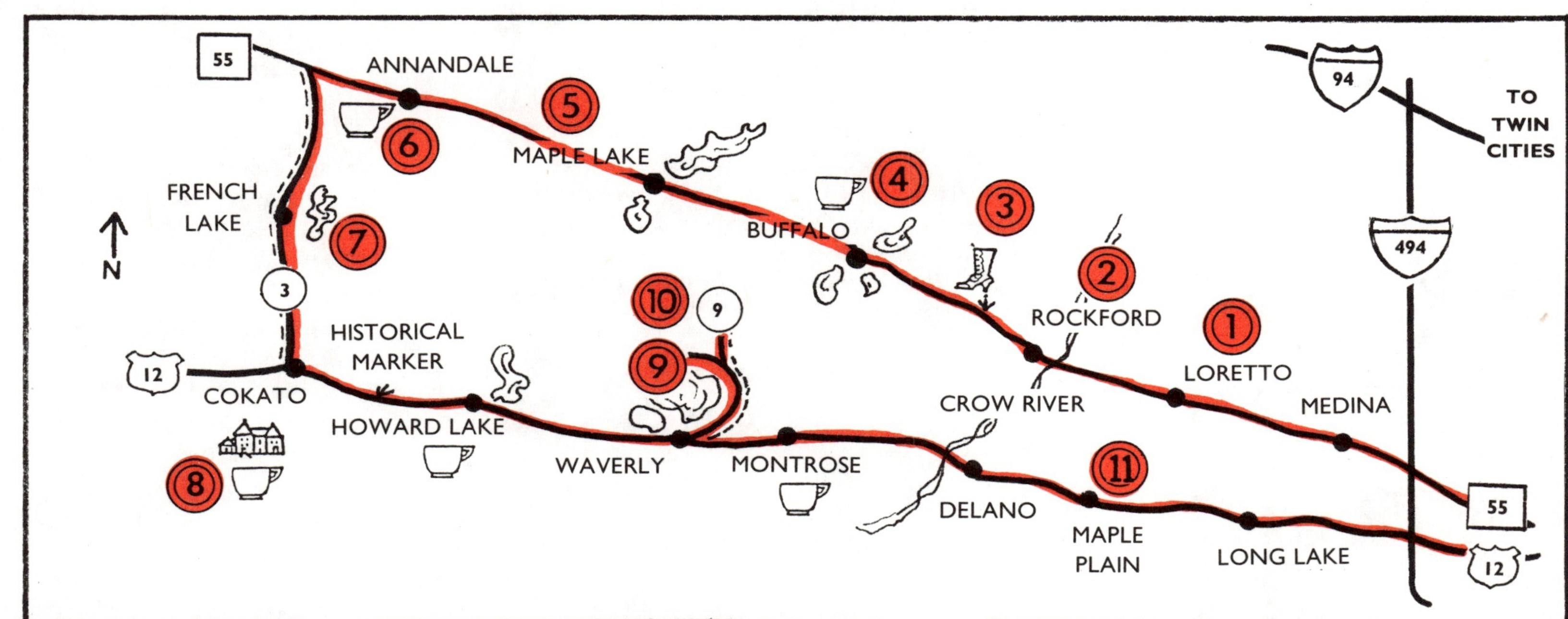

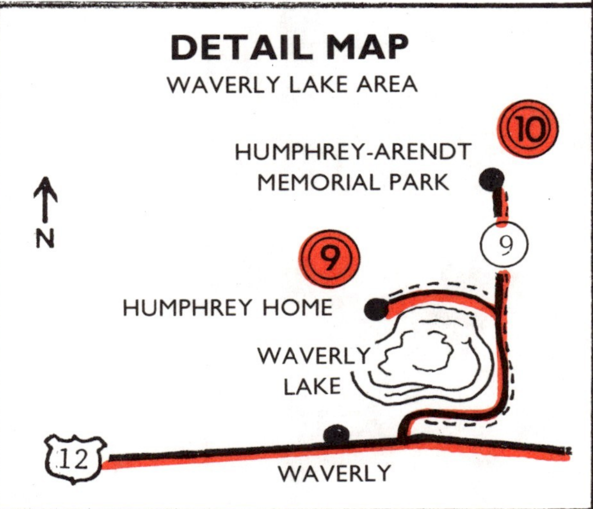

APPROX. TOTAL TOUR MILES 115

INTEREST POINT

FOOD 

HISTORIC SITE 

ANTIQUES 

PARK 

SCENIC ROUTE - - - -

MUSEUM  

TOUR 24 BLANKETS AND BANDITS AN EXCITING DAY

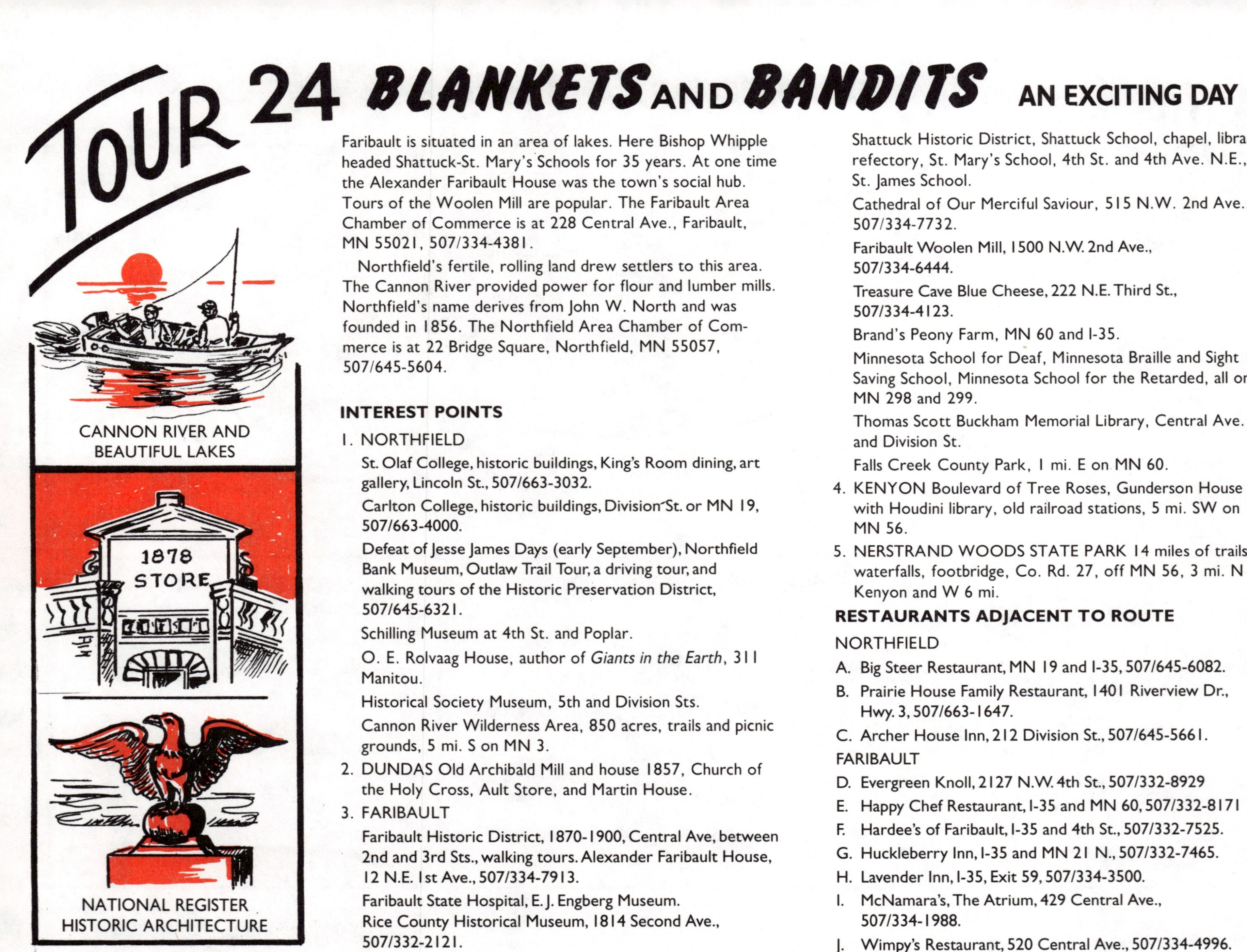

CANNON RIVER AND BEAUTIFUL LAKES

NATIONAL REGISTER HISTORIC ARCHITECTURE

Faribault is situated in an area of lakes. Here Bishop Whipple headed Shattuck-St. Mary's Schools for 35 years. At one time the Alexander Faribault House was the town's social hub. Tours of the Woolen Mill are popular. The Faribault Area Chamber of Commerce is at 228 Central Ave., Faribault, MN 55021, 507/334-4381.

Northfield's fertile, rolling land drew settlers to this area. The Cannon River provided power for flour and lumber mills. Northfield's name derives from John W. North and was founded in 1856. The Northfield Area Chamber of Commerce is at 22 Bridge Square, Northfield, MN 55057, 507/645-5604.

INTEREST POINTS

1. NORTHFIELD

   St. Olaf College, historic buildings, King's Room dining, art gallery, Lincoln St., 507/663-3032.

   Carlton College, historic buildings, Division St. or MN 19, 507/663-4000.

   Defeat of Jesse James Days (early September), Northfield Bank Museum, Outlaw Trail Tour, a driving tour, and walking tours of the Historic Preservation District, 507/645-6321.

   Schilling Museum at 4th St. and Poplar.

   O. E. Rolvaag House, author of *Giants in the Earth*, 311 Manitou.

   Historical Society Museum, 5th and Division Sts.

   Cannon River Wilderness Area, 850 acres, trails and picnic grounds, 5 mi. S on MN 3.

2. DUNDAS Old Archibald Mill and house 1857, Church of the Holy Cross, Ault Store, and Martin House.

3. FARIBAULT

   Faribault Historic District, 1870-1900, Central Ave, between 2nd and 3rd Sts., walking tours. Alexander Faribault House, 12 N.E. 1st Ave., 507/334-7913.

   Faribault State Hospital, E. J. Engberg Museum.
   Rice County Historical Museum, 1814 Second Ave., 507/332-2121.

   Shattuck Historic District, Shattuck School, chapel, library, refectory, St. Mary's School, 4th St. and 4th Ave. N.E., St. James School.

   Cathedral of Our Merciful Saviour, 515 N.W. 2nd Ave., 507/334-7732.

   Faribault Woolen Mill, 1500 N.W. 2nd Ave., 507/334-6444.

   Treasure Cave Blue Cheese, 222 N.E. Third St., 507/334-4123.

   Brand's Peony Farm, MN 60 and I-35.

   Minnesota School for Deaf, Minnesota Braille and Sight Saving School, Minnesota School for the Retarded, all on MN 298 and 299.

   Thomas Scott Buckham Memorial Library, Central Ave. and Division St.

   Falls Creek County Park, 1 mi. E on MN 60.

4. KENYON Boulevard of Tree Roses, Gunderson House with Houdini library, old railroad stations, 5 mi. SW on MN 56.

5. NERSTRAND WOODS STATE PARK 14 miles of trails, waterfalls, footbridge, Co. Rd. 27, off MN 56, 3 mi. N of Kenyon and W 6 mi.

RESTAURANTS ADJACENT TO ROUTE

NORTHFIELD

A. Big Steer Restaurant, MN 19 and I-35, 507/645-6082.

B. Prairie House Family Restaurant, 1401 Riverview Dr., Hwy. 3, 507/663-1647.

C. Archer House Inn, 212 Division St., 507/645-5661.

FARIBAULT

D. Evergreen Knoll, 2127 N.W. 4th St., 507/332-8929

E. Happy Chef Restaurant, I-35 and MN 60, 507/332-8171

F. Hardee's of Faribault, I-35 and 4th St., 507/332-7525.

G. Huckleberry Inn, I-35 and MN 21 N., 507/332-7465.

H. Lavender Inn, I-35, Exit 59, 507/334-3500.

I. McNamara's, The Atrium, 429 Central Ave., 507/334-1988.

J. Wimpy's Restaurant, 520 Central Ave., 507/334-4996.

TOUR 24 FARIBAULT and NORTHFIELD, HISTORY AND TRADITION

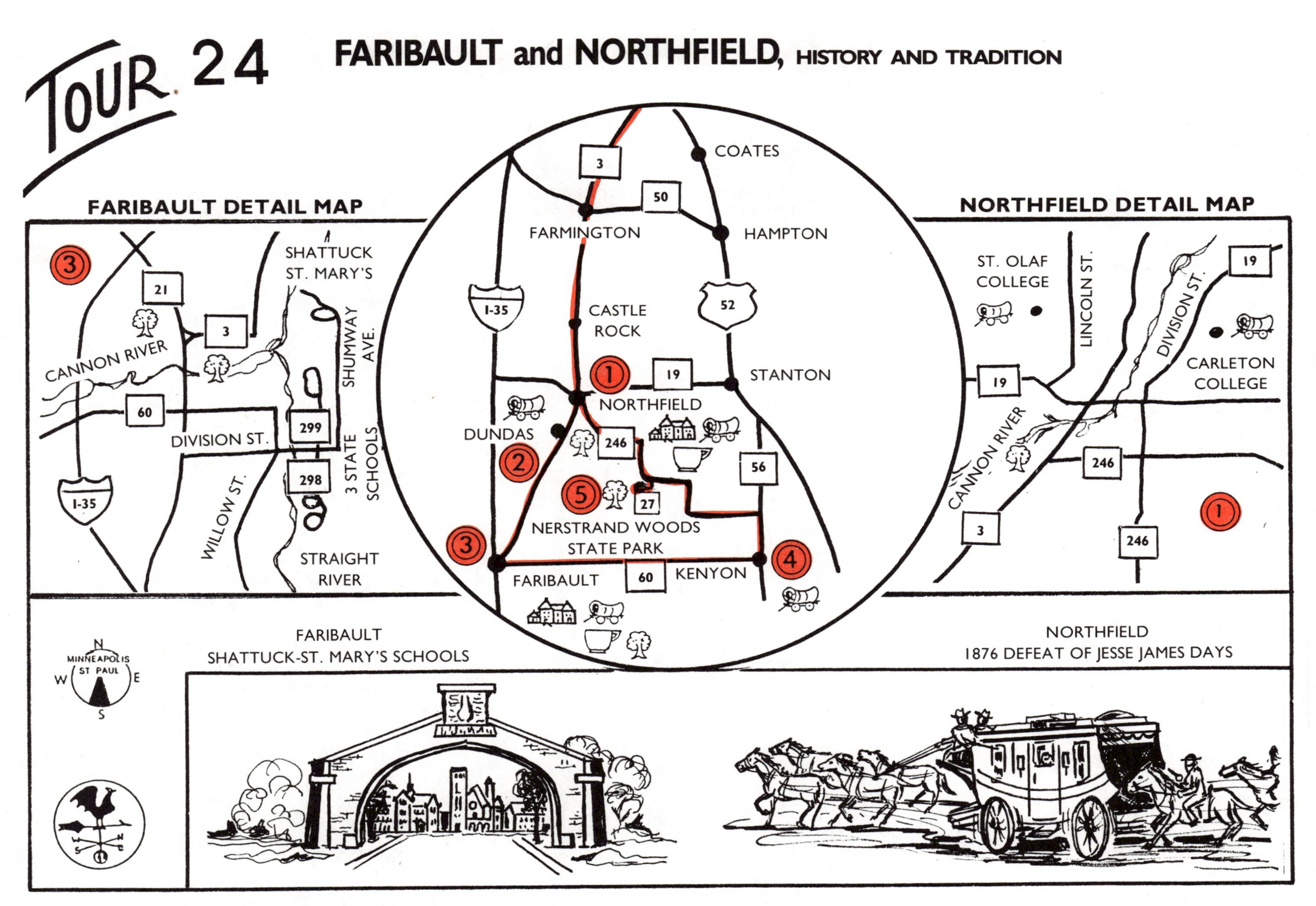

APPROX. TOTAL TOUR MILES  INTEREST POINT  FOOD  HISTORIC SITE   ANTIQUES  PARK SCENIC ROUTE MUSEUM

TOUR 25 PARKLAND AND A GOLD STRIP

WOODLAKE NATURE CENTER
RICHFIELD

JAPANESE GARDEN
BLOOMINGTON

Bloomington, Minnesota's third largest city, and the neighbor city of Richfield are steeped in history. Indian trails, pioneer schools, fishing, fur trade, ample wildlife on river bluffs and verdant valleys all had their role in the early 1880s. Today the two cities area is bustling and thriving with diverse industry and business. Proximity to the airport has created a "Gold Strip" of motels, restaurants and entertainment. Highway I-494 is the boundary between the two communities.

INTEREST POINTS

1. SOUTHTOWN CENTER Begin the tour here, I-494 and Penn Ave. S., Bloomington.
2. THE "GOLD STRIP" Follow I-494 W to get a taste of the choice of restaurants and accommodations available. Turn S on Co. Rd. 18, then turn left on Amsden Road, follow Bush Lake Road and take the left fork or E. Bush Lake Rd.
3. BUSH LAKE PARK Swimming beach, picnic sites, hill trail, 9201 E. Bush Lake Rd., 612/887-9601.
4. RICHARDSON NATURE CENTER Trails, center, 8737 E. Bush Lake Rd., 612/941-7993.
5. HYLAND LAKE SKI AREA and MT. NORMANDALE LAKE PARK Turn S on Chalet Road at 84th St. to the park and to the ski area at 8800 Chalet Rd., 612/835-3923.
6. NORMANDALE COMMUNITY COLLEGE and THE JAPANESE GARDEN. Follow 84th E to France Ave. Turn S to 9700 France Ave., then W on 98th St. to Collegeview Ave., and N to the Japanese Garden. Tours, call 612/830-3923.
7. HYLAND LAKE PARK RESERVE and PICNIC AREA From the Japanese Garden go W on 98th St. to Normandale Blvd., S to Old Shakopee Rd. and N on Bush Lake Rd. to the park. Here is an unusual creative play area with chutes, slides, climbing nets all on a side hill site. There is a lovely center, paddleboats, and fishing dock, 10145 E. Bush Lake Rd. 612/944-9882/941-4362.
8. DRED SCOTT FIELD A many-acre recreation area at 109 Bloomington Ferry Rd.
9. BETHANY FELLOWSHIP A missionary training center, tours, 6820 Auto Club Rd., 612/944-2121.
10. MASONIC HOME Turn N on Normandale Blvd., tours, 11400 Normandale Blvd., 612/881-8665.
11. BLOOMINGTON COMMUNITY ICE GARDEN 3600 W. 98th St., 612/887-9641.
12. BLOOMINGTON CITY HALL, ART CENTER and MUSEUM all at Old Shakopee and Penn Ave. S., tours, 612/887-9645. Also MOIR PARK, trails, picnic sites, 104th St. and Morgan Ave. S., 612/881-5811.
13. MALL OF AMERICA Discover the world's premier retail and entertainment complex that features over 400 specialty shops plus four anchor department stores, Camp Snoopy (seven acres of fun), 30 restaurants – and divided into four distinct theme areas. For information call Mall of America, 2051 Killebrew Drive, Suite 500, Bloomington, MN 55425, 612/851-3675.

    MINNESOTA VALLEY NATIONAL WILDLIFE REFUGE has a center, trails, lookout, bass ponds and wetlands. Follow Old Shakopee to 34th Ave., turn E on 80th St., go to end of road, 4101 E 80th St., 612/854-5900.
14. METROPOLITAN STADIUM SPORTS CENTER Turn W on 494 to Cedar Ave., turn N to 66th St., turn W to see the RICHFIELD ICE ARENA, the POOL and LEGION LAKE PARK all near 66th St. and Portland Ave.
15. WOODLAKE NATURE INTERPRETIVE CENTER Go W on 66th St. to Woodlake Drive (just past Lyndale Ave.) to find nature trails, floating boardwalks and center buildings, 735 Lake Shore Dr., 612/861-4507.

    BARTHOLOMEW HOUSE S to Lyndale Ave. to a historic house, 1853, at 69th St., tours, 612/866-1294. Return to 66th St. and go W to Penn Ave. S. Drive S to Southtown Shopping Center, the starting point.

RESTAURANTS ADJACENT TO ROUTE

There are many fine restaurants along the "Gold Strip," and also on 66th Street and Old Shakopee Road.

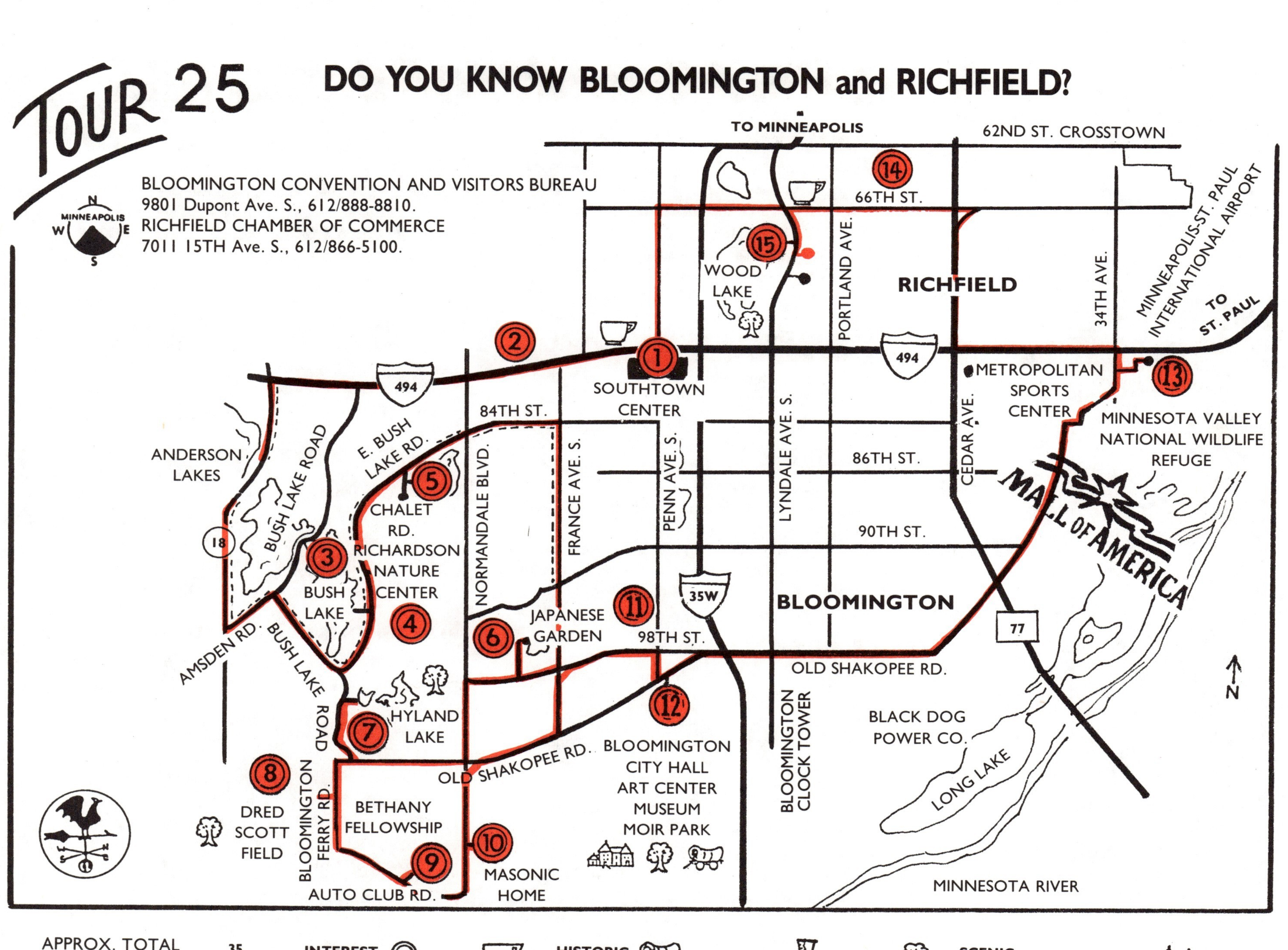
TOUR 25
DO YOU KNOW BLOOMINGTON and RICHFIELD?
BLOOMINGTON CONVENTION AND VISITORS BUREAU
9801 Dupont Ave. S., 612/888-8810.
RICHFIELD CHAMBER OF COMMERCE
7011 15TH Ave. S., 612/866-5100.
MINNEAPOLIS
N
W
E
S
TO MINNEAPOLIS
62ND ST. CROSSTOWN
66TH ST.
WOOD LAKE
PORTLAND AVE.
RICHFIELD
34TH AVE.
MINNEAPOLIS-ST. PAUL INTERNATIONAL AIRPORT
TO ST. PAUL
494
SOUTHTOWN CENTER
METROPOLITAN SPORTS CENTER
MINNESOTA VALLEY NATIONAL WILDLIFE REFUGE
84TH ST.
E. BUSH LAKE RD.
ANDERSON LAKES
BUSH LAKE ROAD
CHALET RD.
RICHARDSON NATURE CENTER
NORMANDALE BLVD.
FRANCE AVE. S.
PENN AVE. S.
LYNDALE AVE. S.
86TH ST.
CEDAR AVE.
MALL OF AMERICA
90TH ST.
18
BUSH LAKE
JAPANESE GARDEN
35W
BLOOMINGTON
98TH ST.
77
AMSDEN RD.
BUSH LAKE ROAD
OLD SHAKOPEE RD.
HYLAND LAKE
BLOOMINGTON CLOCK TOWER
BLACK DOG POWER CO.
OLD SHAKOPEE RD.
BLOOMINGTON CITY HALL
ART CENTER
MUSEUM
MOIR PARK
LONG LAKE
DRED SCOTT FIELD
BLOOMINGTON FERRY RD.
BETHANY FELLOWSHIP
MASONIC HOME
AUTO CLUB RD.
MINNESOTA RIVER
N

APPROX. TOTAL TOUR MILES

35

INTEREST POINT

FOOD

HISTORIC SITE

ANTIQUES

PARK

SCENIC ROUTE

MUSEUM

TOUR 26 GERMAN HERITAGE

SAVOR THE DAY

The idea for New Ulm was born in Germany in 1852. Frederick Beinhorn formed the "Chicago Land Association" which later merged with the "Cincinnati Settlement Society" in America. Today New Ulm is a prospering city that is proud of its German culture and traditions.

You will enjoy discovering the old world charm and will quickly be aware of the German accented names of local shops. Take your time and explore the unusual sights. Climb the Hermann Monument's three-story steps to the lookout tower, visit Domeier's German Store and wander in the streets of historic buildings and homes. The Glockenspiel in Schonlau Plaza is a major New Ulm attraction, A 37-bell carillon is contained in a 45-foot tower and animated historical figurines emerge at noon, 3 p.m. and 5 p.m.

Two exciting festivals are held each year: Heritagefest in late July, which features the play "Herman's Dream," and the Octoberfest which occurs in mid-October. Markers throughout the city recall historic events. The friendly people in the Visitor's Center will supply you with maps and brochures (Third St. N. and Broadway). Historic New Ulm and farm tours may be arranged by contacting the New Ulm Area Chamber of Commerce, Box 384, New Ulm, MN, 56073, 507/354-4217.

INTEREST POINTS

1. CHASKA A romantic town square with a gazebo has old-time charm. Chaska would be a good coffee-break stop.
2. NEW ULM
   Hermann Monument is a 102-foot statue to Herman Arminius who unified the Germanic tribes, Center St. near Summit Ave.

   The Glockenspiel Musical Clock Tower is a freestanding clock-tower with performances by figures as music is played on bells, 4th N. St. and Minnesota St.

   The Brick Sculpture depicts history on a wall, 16 N. Minnesota St.

   The Museum includes a museum-library complex, 27 N. Broadway.

   The Way of the Cross is outdoor stations that depict the events of the crucifixion near a chapel overlooking the valley, 1324 5th S. St.

   Schells Garden, Mansion and Park, 20th S. St. and Payne St.

   A walking tour of historic homes and buildings, historic markers, Dr. Martin Luther College, Steamboat Landing area and park, and cemetery and many quaint shops are a must before you leave New Ulm.

   Flandrau State Park offers high wooded bluffs with picnic grounds, trails and swimming, on the south border of New Ulm.
3. HARKIN-MASSOPUST STORE Check prices and smell the aromas of a century ago, Co. Rd. 21, 8 miles NW of New Ulm, 507/359-9729/697-6321.
4. SWAN LAKE COUNTY PARK On your return you will find a County Park on Swan Lake at Nicollet, and at Arlington is a High Island Scenic Area.

RESTAURANTS ADJACENT TO ROUTE

A. Chaska Bell, Hwy. 212 E., Chaska, 612/448-4098.

B. J'S Family Restaurant, 222 Chestnut St., Chaska, 612/448-4093.

C. Prairie House Family Restaurant, MN 19, Gaylord, 507/237-5936.

D. Glockenspiel Haus Restaurant, 400 N. Minnesota St., New Ulm, 507/354-5593.

E. Hardee's of New Ulm, 622 N. Broadway, New Ulm, 507/369-9312.

F. Heidelberg, 2101 S. Broadway, New Ulm, 507/359-2941.

WORLD FAMOUS GLOCKENSPIEL

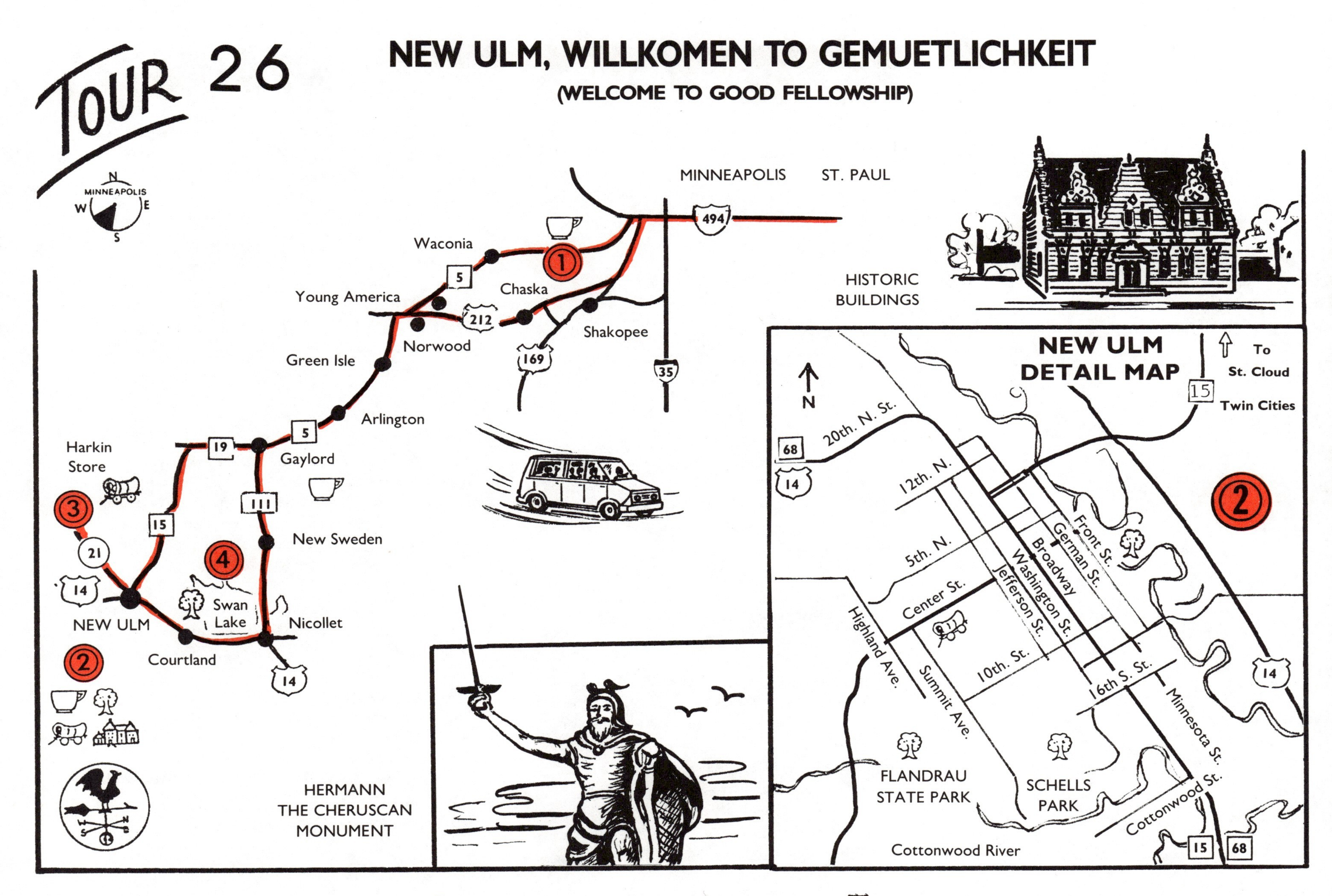

APPROX. TOTAL TOUR MILES 190 · INTEREST POINT · FOOD · HISTORIC SITE · ANTIQUES · PARK · SCENIC ROUTE · MUSEUM

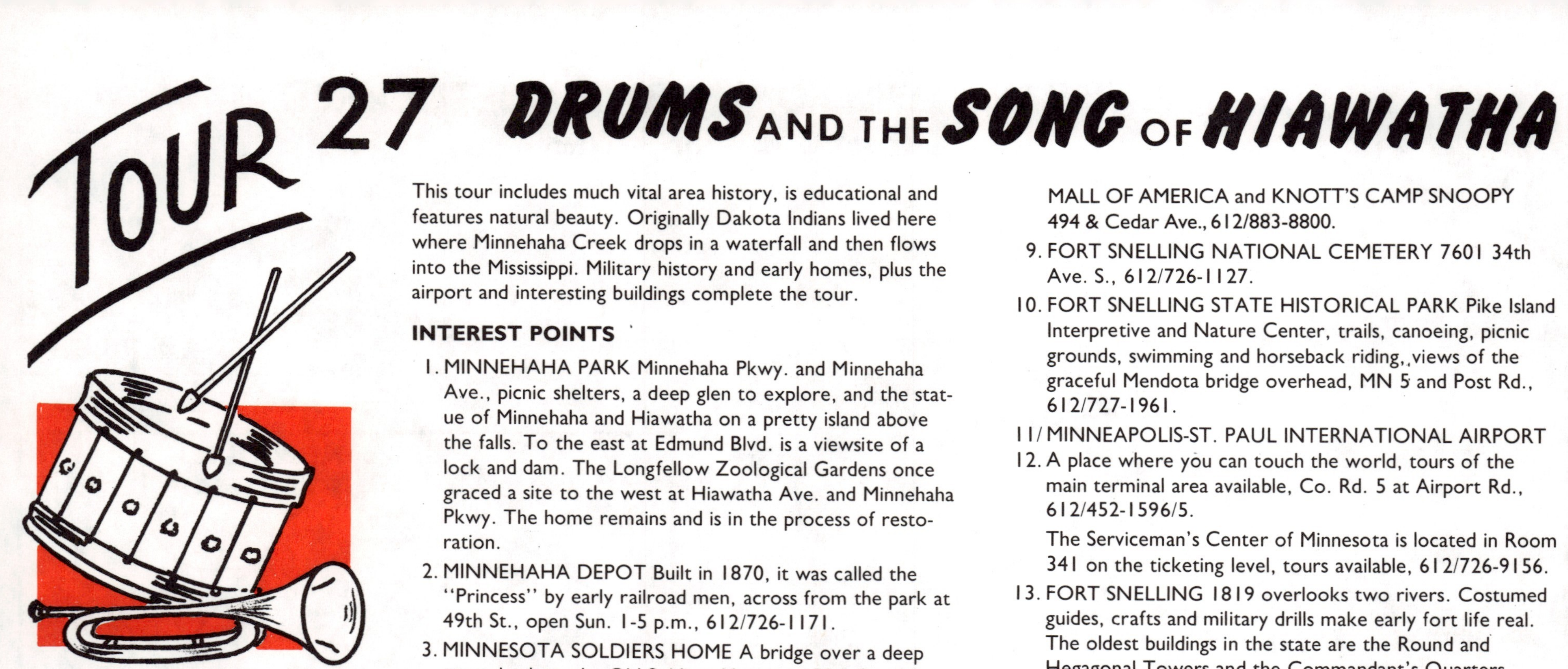

TOUR 27 DRUMS AND THE SONG OF HIAWATHA

This tour includes much vital area history, is educational and features natural beauty. Originally Dakota Indians lived here where Minnehaha Creek drops in a waterfall and then flows into the Mississippi. Military history and early homes, plus the airport and interesting buildings complete the tour.

INTEREST POINTS

1. MINNEHAHA PARK Minnehaha Pkwy. and Minnehaha Ave., picnic shelters, a deep glen to explore, and the statue of Minnehaha and Hiawatha on a pretty island above the falls. To the east at Edmund Blvd. is a viewsite of a lock and dam. The Longfellow Zoological Gardens once graced a site to the west at Hiawatha Ave. and Minnehaha Pkwy. The home remains and is in the process of restoration.
2. MINNEHAHA DEPOT Built in 1870, it was called the "Princess" by early railroad men, across from the park at 49th St., open Sun. 1-5 p.m., 612/726-1171.
3. MINNESOTA SOLDIERS HOME A bridge over a deep gorge leads to the Old Soldiers Home, at 50th St. and Minnehaha.
4. JOHN H. STEVENS HOUSE A small house where Minneapolis was named, Hennepin County organized, and the school district and Agricultural Society formed, 4901 Minnehaha Ave.
5. U.S. VETERANS HOSPITAL A large facility with tours available, 54th St. and 48th Ave. S., 612/725-2000. Drive W on MN 62 and as the road makes a sharp left curve note the fenced-in area where original prairie grasses are preserved.
6. U.S. AIR FORCE AIR GUARD MUSEUM Open Sat. and Sun., S of MN 62 and W of Hiawatha 612/726-9430.
7. MINNESOTA VALLEY NATIONAL WILDLIFE REFUGE Nature center, trails, lookout, off I-494 at 34th Ave., turn left on 80th St., go 3 blocks, 4101 E. 78th St., 612/854-5900.
8. H. H. HUMPHREY INTERNATIONAL CHARTER TERMINAL 34th Ave. S at I-494, 7100 34th Ave. S., 612/726-5800.

   MALL OF AMERICA and KNOTT'S CAMP SNOOPY 494 & Cedar Ave., 612/883-8800.
9. FORT SNELLING NATIONAL CEMETERY 7601 34th Ave. S., 612/726-1127.
10. FORT SNELLING STATE HISTORICAL PARK Pike Island Interpretive and Nature Center, trails, canoeing, picnic grounds, swimming and horseback riding,,views of the graceful Mendota bridge overhead, MN 5 and Post Rd., 612/727-1961.
11/ MINNEAPOLIS-ST. PAUL INTERNATIONAL AIRPORT
12. A place where you can touch the world, tours of the main terminal area available, Co. Rd. 5 at Airport Rd., 612/452-1596/5.

    The Serviceman's Center of Minnesota is located in Room 341 on the ticketing level, tours available, 612/726-9156.
13. FORT SNELLING 1819 overlooks two rivers. Costumed guides, crafts and military drills make early fort life real. The oldest buildings in the state are the Round and Hegagonal Towers and the Commandant's Quarters. Open May-Sept., modest fee, MN 5 and 55, 612/726-1171, Memorial Chapel 612/727-1961.
14. MENDOTA Historic homes in a picturesque river valley town, tours available of the Sibley House 1835, the Faribault House and the DuPois House, also St. Peter's Church, all at Co. Rds. 55 and 13, Sibley House Association, 612/452-1596.
15. VETERANS ADMINISTRATION CENTER Federal building, a beautiful facility, Co. 55 S of MN 62, 612/726-1454.

RESTAURANTS ADJACENT TO THE ROUTE

A. Wooley's Too Restaurant, 7901 34th Ave. S., 612/854-1010 (In The Embassy Suites — Mpls-Airport).

B. The Parker House, Mendota, 612/452-1881.

C. Mariner Restaurant, 1351 Sibley Memorial Dr., 612/452-1830.

D. Garden Restaurant, Mpls./St. Paul International Airport, 612/726-5341.

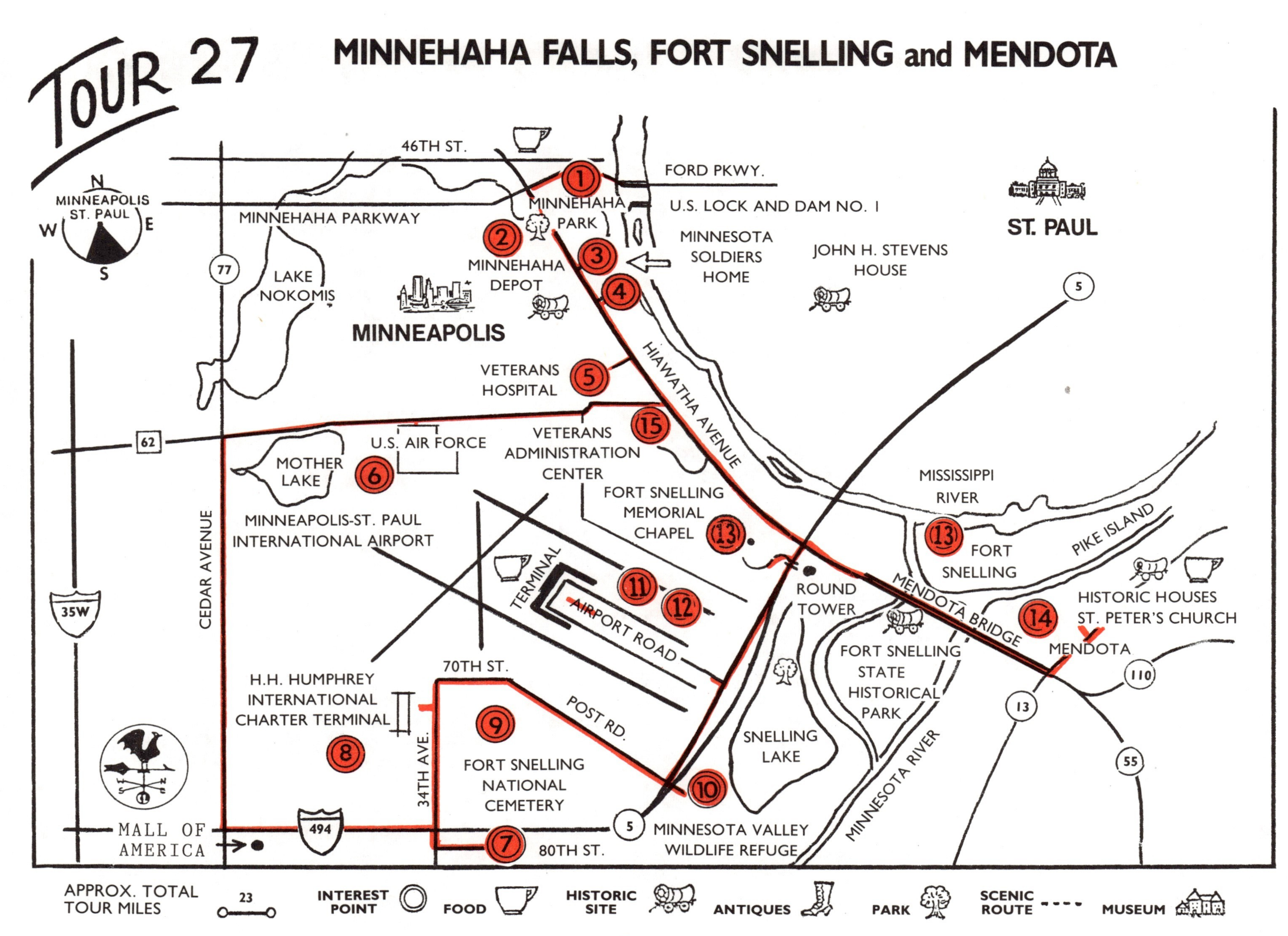
TOUR 27
MINNEHAHA FALLS, FORT SNELLING and MENDOTA
N
MINNEAPOLIS
ST. PAUL
W
E
S
46TH ST.
FORD PKWY.
MINNEHAHA PARKWAY
MINNEHAHA PARK
U.S. LOCK AND DAM NO. 1
ST. PAUL
MINNESOTA SOLDIERS HOME
JOHN H. STEVENS HOUSE
LAKE NOKOMIS
MINNEHAHA DEPOT
MINNEAPOLIS
77
5
VETERANS HOSPITAL
HIAWATHA AVENUE
62
U.S. AIR FORCE
VETERANS ADMINISTRATION CENTER
MOTHER LAKE
MISSISSIPPI RIVER
FORT SNELLING MEMORIAL CHAPEL
MINNEAPOLIS-ST. PAUL INTERNATIONAL AIRPORT
FORT SNELLING
PIKE ISLAND
CEDAR AVENUE
TERMINAL
AIRPORT ROAD
ROUND TOWER
MENDOTA BRIDGE
HISTORIC HOUSES
ST. PETER'S CHURCH
MENDOTA
35W
FORT SNELLING STATE HISTORICAL PARK
110
13
70TH ST.
H.H. HUMPHREY INTERNATIONAL CHARTER TERMINAL
POST RD.
SNELLING LAKE
MINNESOTA RIVER
55
34TH AVE.
FORT SNELLING NATIONAL CEMETERY
MALL OF AMERICA
494
80TH ST.
MINNESOTA VALLEY WILDLIFE REFUGE
1
2
3
4
5
6
7
8
9
10
11
12
13
14
15
APPROX. TOTAL TOUR MILES
23
INTEREST POINT
FOOD
HISTORIC SITE
ANTIQUES
PARK
SCENIC ROUTE
MUSEUM

TOUR 28 LUMBERJACKS AND GANGSTERS

INDIAN HERITAGE

DEVIL'S CHAIR
ST. CROIX DALLES

Wisconsin is endowed with unusual beauty in majestic scenery of glacial ridges, gorges and deep ravines. Blue waters sparkle in lakes, rivers and peaceful streams. State parks, historic sites, recreational opportunities abound. The history of pioneer days, fur traders and loggers is preserved for present-day exploring. A wonderful day may be enjoyed just a short distance from the Twin Cities.

INTEREST POINTS

1. ST. CROIX FALLS What a versatility of attractions are available here. The Ice Age Interpretive Center has exhibits that tell the story of the glaciers with dramatic presentations. Interstate Park's role is explained in the Ice Age Scientific Reserve. In the area are the Glacial Pot Hole trail, Eagle's Peak, the St. Croix National Scenic Riverway Museum, a scenic overlook, antiques, cheese shops, the Lion's Park and picnic grounds. Wannigan Days, held in June, recall lumberjack legends and are lively with pie socials, parades and art shows. Call 612/465-6315 for exact date and details. River boat trips through gorges having unusual formations are appealing. Watch for the Old Man of the Dalles, the most outstanding natural rock face, the Devil's Chair, Lion's Head, Turk's Head and the huge stone cross for which the St. Croix (Sacred Cross) was named by early French explorers. These can be seen only by boat, boat tours, 612/291-7980. St. Croix Falls Chamber of Commerce, 612/483-3929.
2. SPOONER Department of Natural Resources Fish Hatchery (S of town on US 63), world's largest warm water fish hatchery, picnic grounds. Agate Artifacts with rock displays, 2 mi. N on US 63.
3. TREGO St. Croix National Riverway Information Center, N edge of town on the beautiful Namekagon River. A deer farm where you can feed and pet deer, 3 mi. S on US 63.
4. HAYWARD Step back in time to the lumberjack era in a restored logging community. Visit the National Fresh Water Fishery Hall of Fame where you can go inside a huge fish. Windmill Square has quaint shops for browsing. Have lunch in a bunkhouse and tour the museum. For water-lovers, there is tubing on the Namekagon River or lovely boat cruises on the lake. Historyland is a reconstructed Chippewa Indian village and old-time settlement, 715/634-4811.
5. AL CAPONE'S NORTHWOODS RETREAT THE HIDEOUT is at Couderay. Formerly closed and tightly guarded, it now has tours of this 400-acre roaring 20's gangland hideout. Where else can you see such an unusual place having a jail cell, gun tower, main lodge and bunk-house? Follow the detail map to find the Hideout, tours, 715/945-2746.
6. RICE LAKE'S INDIAN MOUNDS PARK is an archeological site of burial grounds that shows how Ojibway Indians honored their dead.
7 CAMERON The Barron County Historical Society Museum has 21 buildings depicting homes and shops of Barron County pioneers (W of town on Co. Rd. W).

RESTAURANTS ADJACENT TO THE ROUTE

A. Chisago House, 311 Bench St., Taylors Falls, MN, 612/465-5245.

B. Dalles House, Junction WI 35 and US 8, St. Croix Falls, WI, 612/291-7980.

C. Historyland Logging Camp Cook Shanty, History Lane at Co. Rd. B, Hayward, WI, 715/634-4811.

D. Al Capone's The Hideout, Couderay, WI, 715/945-2746.

E. Turtle Lake Inn Supper Club, 3 mi. E of Turtle Lake, WI, 715/945-2746.

F. Trappers Inn, 3 mi. W at US 8 and MN 95, Chisago City, MN 612/465-5121.

TOUR 28

ST. CROIX FALLS, HAYWARD and THE HIDEOUT

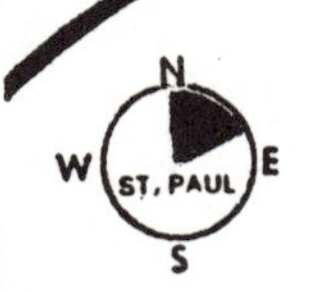

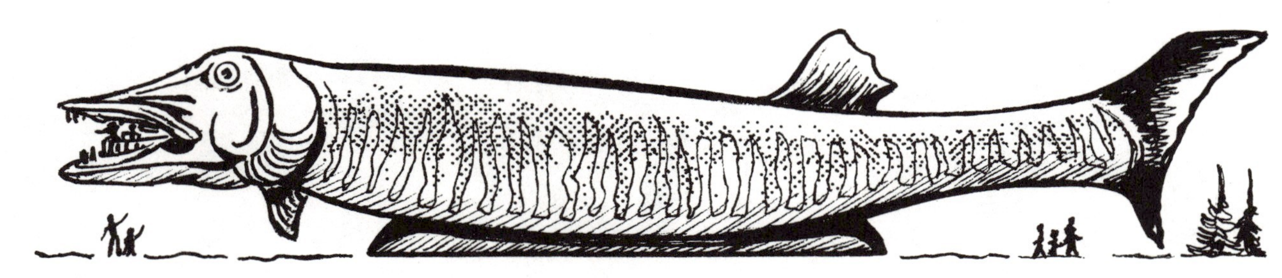

NATIONAL FRESH WATER
FISHING HALL OF FAME
HAYWARD, WISCONSIN

THE CROSS

OLD MAN
OF THE DALLES

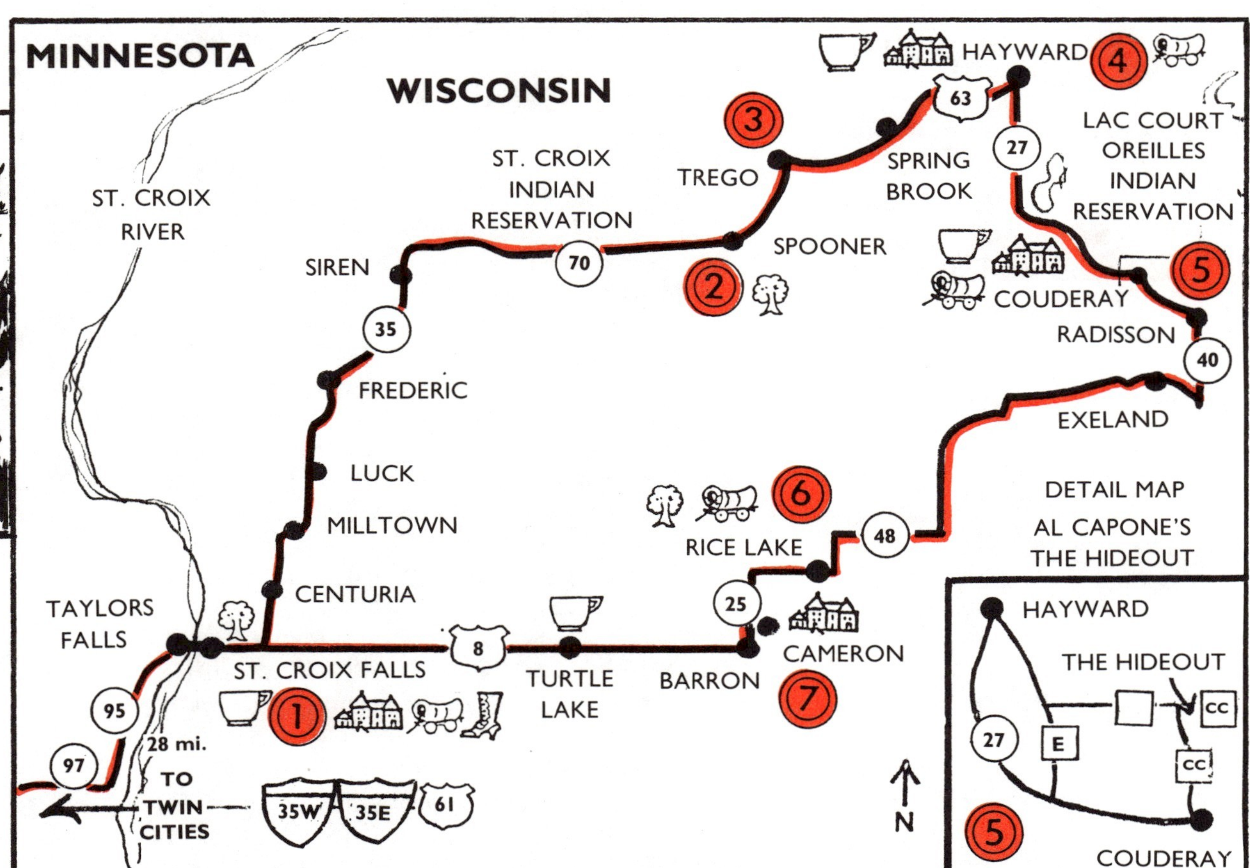

APPROX. TOTAL TOUR MILES   200

INTEREST POINT  FOOD

HISTORIC SITE 

ANTIQUES 

PARK 

SCENIC ROUTE 

MUSEUM 

TOUR 29 WHERE ARE ELYSIAN AND SAKATAH?

WORLD'S BULLHEAD CAPITAL

MEMORY MANOR COUNTRY STORE

Where is Elysian? Where are the "Singing Hills"? Where is the World's Kolaky Capital? What Town has Bullhead Days? Where is Memory Manor? Where can you dine in old-world atmosphere or spend an entire day at a farm on a lake? If you follow the route of this tour, the answers to all these questions will be revealed.

INTEREST POINTS

1. Head S on I-35 and exit at Co. Rd. 70. Turn E to discover a MCDONALD'S MEGASTOP, one of the first in the nation. It's a good place for a cup of coffee and a "Danish." Turn S on the service road or Co. Rd. 46 and watch for
2. HOT SAMS on the right side of the road. A caboose, antique trucks and a house full of collectables are here.
3. Continue S on the service road to the Elko-New Market exit, cross over I-35 and turn S to re-enter I-35. Turn W on MN 60 toward Waterville. There is a VISITOR'S CENTER AT MORRISTOWN. You wil be driving parallel to the 42-mile SINGING HILLS STATE TRAIL. A sign directs to SAKATAH LAKE STATE PARK. The park fee is $3.00 and it is worth it just to drive through a beautiful, serene, 842-acre park with virgin woods, picnic sites and water access. Sakatah means "Singing Hills." Call 612/362-4438 or write Sakatah Lake State Park, Rte. 2, Box 19, Waterville, MN 56096 for a brochure.
4. WATERVILLE is the Bullhead Capital of the world and celebrates this title in June. The MINNESOTA FISH HATCHERY and the ALEXANDER FARIBAULT FUR TRADING POST SITE (on Co. Rd. 14) are attractions here. The Waterville Chamber of Commerce, R.R. 2, Box 92A, Waterville MN, 56096, 612/362-8403 has information about the 50 lakes in the area.
5. ELYSIAN (pronounced Eh-*lee*-zee-ann) is the home of two wildlife artists and their work is displayed at the LESUEUR COUNTY HISTORICAL MUSEUM, one block W of MN 60 on Second St., 612/362-8350. A rest stop is on MN 60 in a railroad depot. A CITY PARK is on Elysian Lake. A side trip on Co. Rd. 13, N of town, takes you to the
6. GELDNER SAW MILL, an operating steam-powered mill at Cleveland.
7. At MADISON LAKE is the MEMORY MANOR COUNTRY STORE, a vintage 12-room bank building filled with beautiful collectables. The store is on Main St., 507/267-4381.
8. MONTGOMERY is the World's KOLAKY CAPITAL and celebrates with zeinicky and vomachke (ethnic foods) in July. Write City Clerk of Montgomery, P.O. Box 76, Montgomery, MN, 56069 or call 612/364-8888. A side trip on Co. Rd. 26 leads to Richter Woods.
9. NEW PRAGUE has three major attractions. The ST. WENSELAUS CHURCH is on Main St. SCHUMACHER'S HOTEL RESTAURANT has Czechoslovakian/German food. CEDAR LAKE FARM is N of New Prague at 400 W. 260th St., 56071, 612/758-2284. Family fun with hayrides, boating, animals and barbecued chicken is featured. Return on Co. Rd. 19 to I-35 after a day in kolaky and bullhead country.

RESTAURANTS ADJACENT TO ROUTE

A. McDonald's MC Stop, I-35 and Co. Rd. 70., 612/469-6112.

B. Sportsman's Lounge and Supper Club, 22 E. Main St., Waterville, 612/362-4475.

C. Greenwood Supper Club, on Co. Rd. 130, 2 miles W of Elysian on Lake Francis, 507/267-4381.

D. The Barn, MN 60 E., Madison Lake, 507/243-3434.

E. Schumacher's New Prague Hotel, 212 W. Main St., New Prague, 612/758-2133 or metro line 612/445-7285.

TOUR 29 WATERVILLE, ELYSIAN, MADISON LAKE, and NEW PRAGUE

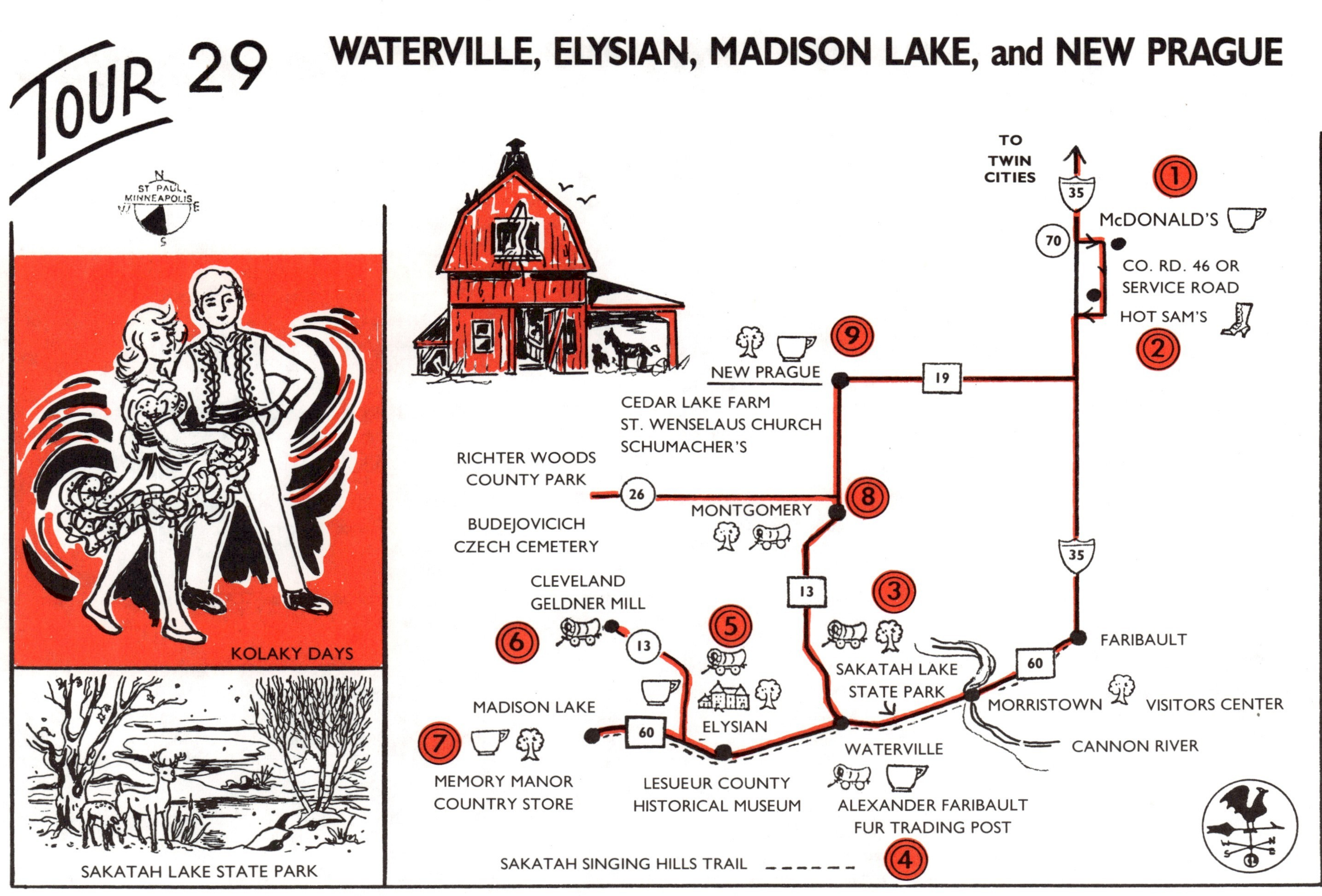

APPROX. TOTAL TOUR MILES 135 | INTEREST POINT | FOOD | HISTORIC SITE | ANTIQUES | PARK | SCENIC ROUTE | MUSEUM

TOUR 30 SCENIC ROADS AND FLYING CLOUDS

FLYING CLOUD AIRPORT

EDINA ART CENTER

EDINA and EDEN PRAIRIE How well are you acquainted with these two cities? Both have curving roads and the tranquility of a suburb, yet are close to the amenities of larger cities. Each has a major shopping center, many parks and a balance of residents, recreation, education and business. Edina was named for Edinburgh, Scotland. Single family homes now are neighbors to business and shopping centers. Eden Prairie was named after Elizabeth Elliot, a journalist, called it a "garden of Eden." This city is growing rapidly, yet has a reminder of the past evident in a pioneer Indian and military trail.

INTEREST POINTS

1. SOUTHDALE SHOPPING CENTER The original of the enclosed malls can be reached from 62nd St., Crosstown or I-494 at 66th St. and France Ave., 612/922-4400.
2. SOUTHDALE HENNEPIN AREA LIBRARY A large, modern facility, just S on York Ave. S. at 7001 York, 612/830-4900.
3. EDINBOROUGH PARK Open to the public with a pool, ice rink, track, and much greenery all under glass, 7700 York Ave., 612/893-9890.

   CENTENNIAL LAKES A lakeside retreat, restaurants, walking paths by lake. 7499 York Ave., Edina, 612/893-9890.
4. LAKE CORNELIA PARK Drive N on MN 100 to 62nd St. Crosstown and exit on Valley View Rd., go S one block to the park entrance, walking paths, pool and picnic shelters, 612/927-9829.
5. EDINA ART CENTER Go W on the 62nd St. Crosstown Service Rd. and follow the signs (N end of park), tours, 4701 W. 64th St., 612/929-4555.
6. 50TH AND FRANCE Fashion, food and fun shops.
7. EDINA HISTORICAL CENTER Old Cahill School, Grange Hall, local history and Wooddale Museum, just E of 50th St. and MN 100, 612/927-8861.
8. BRAEMER PARK, ARENA, and PAVILLION Drive S from 50th St. on Vernon Ave., then S on Gleason Rd. to the park which has facilities for archery, golf, ice skating, gun range, platform tennis and more, 6344 Dewey Hill Rd., 612/941-1322.
9. MINNESOTA VIKINGS WINTER PARK A large Viking boat greets you here. Drive through to see this complex; reach it by driving N from Braemer Park to Valley View Rd., cross the bridge over MN 100 and turn S on Washington Ave., then S to Viking Dr.
10. EDEN PRAIRIE CENTER Take Viking Dr. to US 169-212 to just S of the junction with I-494. A large shopping center has interesting shops and food choices.
11. HENNEPIN COUNTY VO-TECH Tours are available of classrooms, solarium, gardens that are nationally recognized. The Eden Prairie Campus is S on Flying Cloud Dr. (US169-212), 612/944-2222.
12. PAX CHRISTI CATHOLIC COMMUNITY A beautiful modern design facility has tours available. Go S on Flying Cloud Dr. to Pioneer Trail, then E to 12100 Pioneer Trail, 612/941-3150.
13. FLYING CLOUD AIRPORT The Planes of Fame Air Museum has a collection of World War II aircraft. Go W on Pioneer Trail to 14771 Pioneer Trail (Co. Rd. 1), 612/941-2633/471-8344.
14. Go W on Pioneer Trail to STARING LAKE PARK, then continue to Co. Rd. 4, turn S to a historic spring in a wooded setting.
15. EDEN PRAIRIE COMMUNITY CENTER A large new building with a 17,000-square-foot ice rink, pool, meeting rooms and more. Go S from the spring to Flying Cloud Rd., turn W to Eden Prairie Rd., than N to 16700 Valley Rd., 612/937-8727. Follow Valley View N to 62nd St. to return to your starting point.

RESTAURANTS ADJACENT TO ROUTE

EDINA

A. Southdale Shopping Center has a number of restaurants, 66th St. and France Ave. S., 612/922-4400.

EDEN PRAIRIE

B. Eden Prairie Center has a number of food choices, I-94 and Flying Cloud Road.

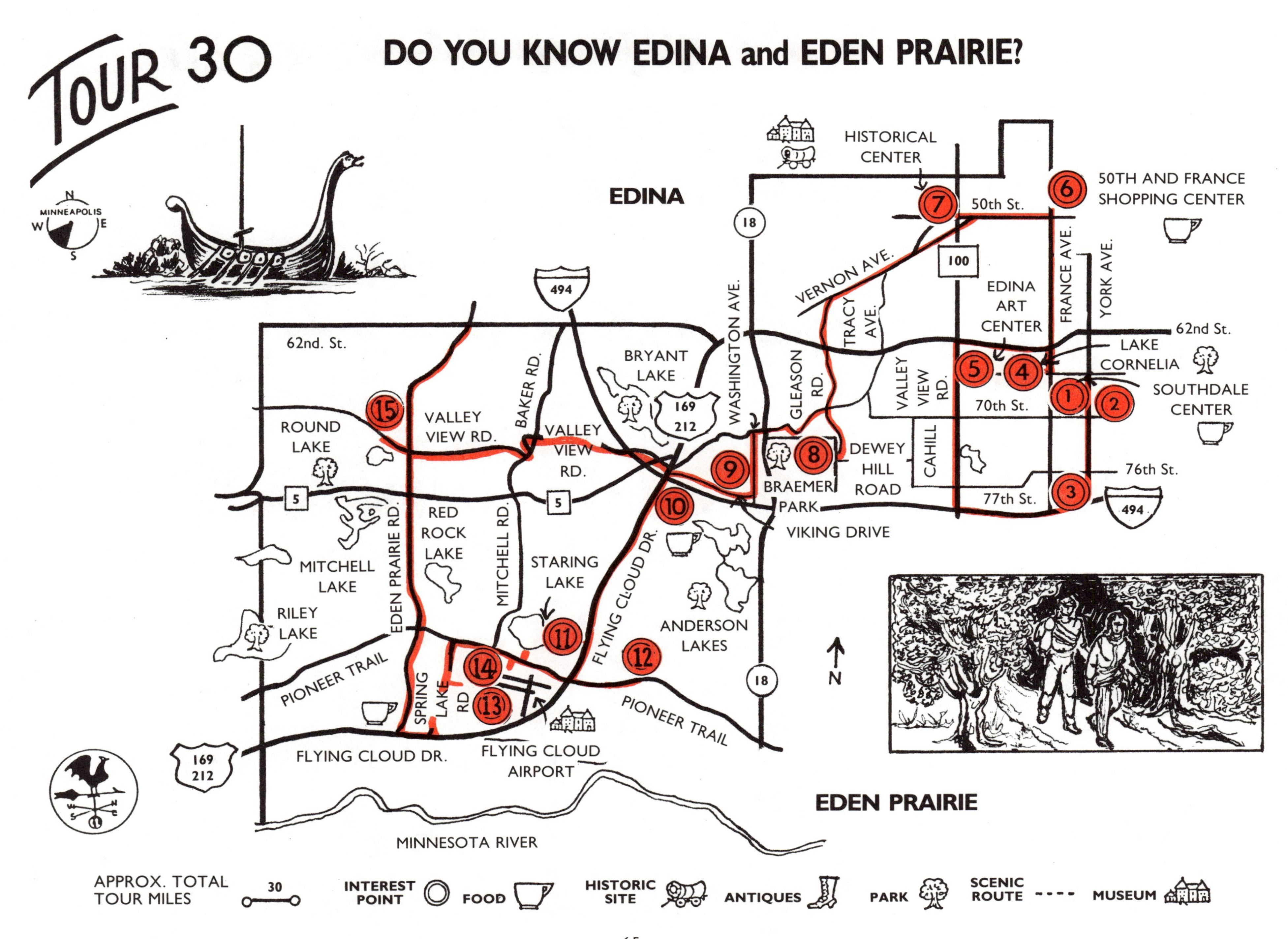
TOUR 30
DO YOU KNOW EDINA and EDEN PRAIRIE?
MINNEAPOLIS
N
W
E
S
EDINA
HISTORICAL CENTER
50TH AND FRANCE SHOPPING CENTER
50th St.
18
100
494
VERNON AVE.
TRACY AVE.
EDINA ART CENTER
FRANCE AVE.
YORK AVE.
62nd St.
LAKE CORNELIA
SOUTHDALE CENTER
62nd. St.
BRYANT LAKE
WASHINGTON AVE.
GLEASON RD.
VALLEY VIEW RD.
70th St.
BAKER RD.
169
212
ROUND LAKE
VALLEY VIEW RD.
DEWEY HILL ROAD
CAHILL
BRAEMER PARK
76th St.
77th St.
5
VIKING DRIVE
RED ROCK LAKE
MITCHELL RD.
EDEN PRAIRIE RD.
STARING LAKE
MITCHELL LAKE
RILEY LAKE
FLYING CLOUD DR.
ANDERSON LAKES
PIONEER TRAIL
SPRING LAKE RD
PIONEER TRAIL
FLYING CLOUD DR.
FLYING CLOUD AIRPORT
EDEN PRAIRIE
MINNESOTA RIVER
APPROX. TOTAL TOUR MILES
30
INTEREST POINT
FOOD
HISTORIC SITE
ANTIQUES
PARK
SCENIC ROUTE
MUSEUM

TOUR 31 TWO TOWERING RIVER BLUFFS

WHITEWATER WILDLIFE AREA

This tour highlights two river cities, Winona and La Crosse, and two majestic bluffs, Sugar Loaf and Grandad. Sugar Loaf is 554 feet above Winona and served as a guiding landmark for river pilots in early history. Grandad Bluff affords a view of three states from its 600-foot height. This tour begins at Weaver, Minnesota.

INTEREST POINTS

1. WEAVER The Noble Studio and Art Galleries.
2. WHITEWATER STATE PARK Enjoy this 1,000-acre unspoiled natural wilderness walled in by limestone cliffs, with trails, trout fishing, swimming, horseback riding and historic sites. CARLEY STATE PARK and WHITEWATER STATE PARK both can be reached on Co. Rd. 2.
3. ST. CHARLES has gladiola gardens and a 1905 red schoolhouse.
4. On US 14 LEWISTON The Arches Museum of Pioneer Life is named for the railroad bridge arches nearby.
   STOCKTON An 1800 water-powered mill is still in operation here in a lovely setting.
5. WINONA
   JULIUS C. WILKIE STEAMBOAT CENTER A dry-docked wooden hull steamer depicts Minnesota steamboating and includes a grand salon and an open air restaurant, at the foot of Main St. on the Mississippi River, 507/452-2272.
   WINONA PRINCESS EXCURSION BOAT Memorable riverboat excursions are available at the end of Walnut St. in Levee Park, 507/454-5315/452-8922.
   GARVIN HEIGHTS SCENIC OUTLOOK An awesome view of the valley, Huff St. to Garvin Heights Rd.
   LAKE WINONA Here you will find rose gardens, bandshell and gazebo, Huff St. and US 61.
   WINONA KNITTING MILLS 910 E. Second St., tours.
   WINONA COUNTY HISTORICAL SOCIETY 160 Johnson St., The Armory, 507/454-2733.
   THE WATKINS COMPANY 150 Liberty St., tours.
   WINONA AREA CHAMBER OF COMMERCE has maps for historic homes, architecture, park and museum locations, 168 Second St., Winona, MN 55987, 507/452-2272.
6. On US 61
   HOMER The Bunnell House, built in 1850, is Gothic Revival style, May-Sept., fee, interpretive tours, Homer and Mathilde Sts.
   PICKWICK MILL An interpretive center representing milling history, turn right at La Moille on Co. Rd. 7 to Pickwick, write Box 645, Winona, MN 55987.
   O.L. KIPP STATE PARK Picnic grounds, trails and camping, junction of I-90 and US 61.
7. LA CRESCENT The Apple Blossom Capitol has a beautiful Hiawathaland Apple Blossom Drive.
8. LA CROSSE
   GRANDAD BLUFF The tallest of the bluffs is reached from US 61 and Main Street, then E to Losey, right fork.
   LA CROSSE QUEEN Riverboat sightseeing trips, at 328 S. Front St., La Crosse, WI, 54601, 608/784-2893.
   HIAWATHA A 25-foot statue at Riverside Park, State St. at the Mississippi River.
   SWARTHOUT MUSEUM 9th and Main Sts., 608/782-1980.
   PUMP HOUSE REGIONAL ART CENTER 119 King St., 608/785-1434.
   LA CROSSE AREA CONVENTION AND VISITORS BUREAU has maps, city park information and historic site locations, P.O. Box 1895, Riverside Park, La Crosse, WI 54601, 608/782-2366.
9. Three Wisconsin Parks are fun to explore:
   PERROT STATE PARK at Centerville, MERRICK STATE PARK at Fountain City, BUENA-VISTA PARK at Alma.

RESTAURANTS ADJACENT TO ROUTE

A. Zach's On The Track, 129 W. Third St., Winona, MN, 507/454-6939.

B. Hot Fish Shop, US 61 and MN 43, Winona, MN, 507/452-5002.

C. Beier's Family Restaurant, 405 US 14, Winona, MN, 507/452-3390.

D. The Freight House, 107 Vine St., La Crosse, WI, 608/784-6211.

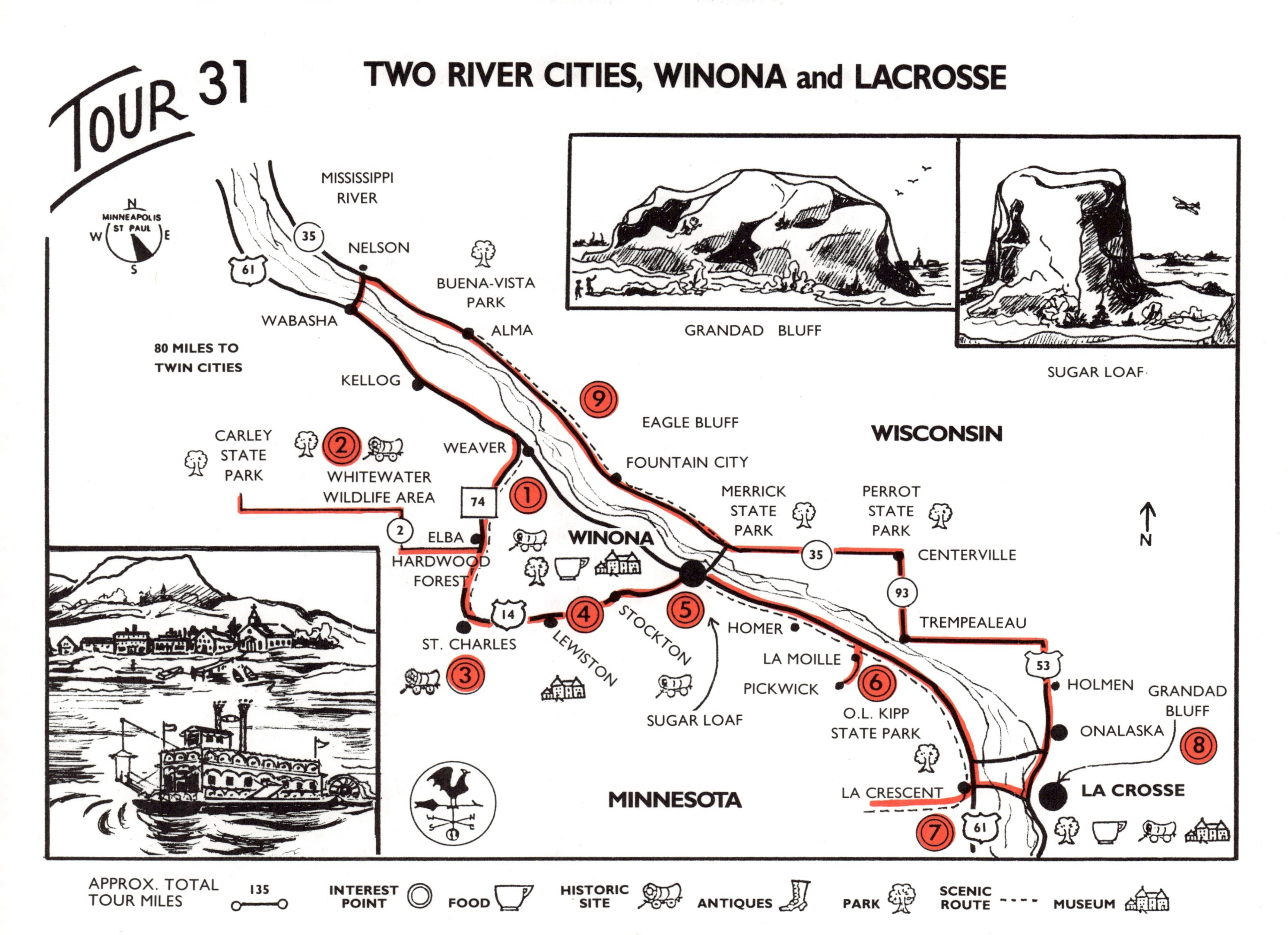

TOUR 31
TWO RIVER CITIES, WINONA and LACROSSE
N
MINNEAPOLIS
ST PAUL
W
E
S
MISSISSIPPI RIVER
35
61
NELSON
BUENA-VISTA PARK
WABASHA
ALMA
80 MILES TO TWIN CITIES
KELLOG
9
EAGLE BLUFF
CARLEY STATE PARK
2
WEAVER
WHITEWATER WILDLIFE AREA
FOUNTAIN CITY
1
74
2
ELBA
WINONA
HARDWOOD FOREST
14
4
STOCKTON
5
ST. CHARLES
LEWISTON
3
HOMER
SUGAR LOAF
GRANDAD BLUFF
SUGAR LOAF
WISCONSIN
MERRICK STATE PARK
PERROT STATE PARK
35
CENTERVILLE
93
TREMPEALEAU
LA MOILLE
PICKWICK
6
O.L. KIPP STATE PARK
53
HOLMEN
ONALASKA
GRANDAD BLUFF
8
LA CROSSE
LA CRESCENT
MINNESOTA
7
61
N
APPROX. TOTAL TOUR MILES
135
INTEREST POINT
FOOD
HISTORIC SITE
ANTIQUES
PARK
SCENIC ROUTE
MUSEUM

TOUR 32 BOARDWALKS AND MEMORIES

WASIOJA CIVIL WAR RECRUITING STATION

MANTORVILLE'S FAMOUS BOARDWALK

This southwestern plains tour offers a chain of delightful towns with a wealth of things to do. There are legends and festivals, history and a ghost town, old mansions and museums filled with reminders of the past. Towns grew or declined depending on whether the railroad came their way. Markers by roadsides show where hamlets flourished and then faded away. Mantorville, the focal destination, is a visitor's delight. Where else can you find a mile of boardwalk inscribed with donor's names?

INTEREST POINTS

1. BERNE Where is Berne, the town? It's really *not*. But if a letter is sent to Berne, the post office will deliver it to the Zwingli Church. This is a Swiss heritage area and comes alive once a year with yodeling, alphorns and cowbells. The Swissfest is the second Tues. in Aug., 2 p.m. and 8 p.m. program times. Contact: Mrs. W. Agerter, West Concord, MN 55985.
2. WASIOJA This quaint ghost town has a Civil War recruiting station, a schoolhouse and ruins of a seminary, W on Co. Rd. 16 (before Mantorville).
3. MANTORVILLE Begin a walking tour (maps available at any shop) with the following: Hubbell House, 507/635-2331; Restoration House; Dodge County Court House Museum, 507/635-5531; The Grand Old Mansion, 507/635-3231. The Historic Opera House has melodramas on weekends June-Aug., 507/635-5420. There is a Little House on the Hill, and picnicking at Riverside Park on the Zumbro River. Marigold Days are held on the weekend following Labor Day. The Winter Carnival is the first full weekend in January. Mantorville Tour Center, Box 246, Mantorville, MN 55955, and the Dodge County Historical Society, Box 433, Mantorville, MN 55955, 507/635-5508.
4. AUSTIN The Mower County Historical Center has Indian, pioneer and railroad exhibits, June-Aug., 12th St. S.W., 507/437-2981/433-1886, free. The Jay C. Hormel Nature Center and Interpretive Center has 178 acres with trails, 1304 21st St. N.E., 507/437-7519, open year-round sunrise to sunset daily, free.
5. ALBERT LEA The Freeborn County Pioneer Village is a restored village open June-Aug., donation, 1031 N. Bridge St., 507/373-8003. The Helmer Myre State Park has acres of virgin prairie with hiking trails and an interpretive center. Lovely lakes are within the city.
6. WASECA Clear Lake, LeSueur River and Courthouse Park make Waseca a restful spot. Native woodlands and a University of Minnesota Experiment Station welcome visitors. Minnesota's FARMAMERICA is a dynamic living history interpretive center dedicated to agriculture, Waseca Area Chamber of Commerce, 123 N. State St., Waseca, MN 56903, 507/835-3260.
7. OWATONNA was named for an Indian princess who came here to drink the mineral water to cure her illness; a statue of her stands at Mineral Springs Park. A beautiful building, Northwestern National Bank was designed by Louis Sullivan and is a symphony of detail and radiant color. The Village of Yesterday, S of Owatonna, has Pioneer buildings and a locomotive that legend says was engineered by Casey Jones, I-35, exit 42, June-Aug., 18th St. S.W., 507/451-7813.

RESTAURANTS ADJACENT TO ROUTE

MANTORVILLE

A. Hubbell House, Inc., MN 57 and US 14, 507/635-2331.

DODGE CENTER

B. C.D. Kirkpatrick and Co., US 14 W., 507/374-9300.

AUSTIN

C. Tolly's Time Out, 100 14th St. S.W., 507/433-6098.

D. The Wagon Wheel, US 218 S., 507/433-6498.

ALBERT LEA

E. Standard Cafe, MN 16 and US 65 E., 507/373-7747.

F. Trumble's, 1811 E. Main, 507/373-2638.

WASECA

G. Happy Chef Restaurant, MN 13 N., 507/835-2624.

OWATONNA

H. Happy Chef Restaurant, I-35 and US 14, 507/451-6831.

I. Perkins Family Restaurant, 1200 I-35, 507/451-6831.

TOUR 32 MANTORVILLE, ALBERT LEA, OWATONNA and AUSTIN

N
MINNEAPOLIS
ST PAUL
W E
S

ANTIQUES

HISTORY

494
TO TWIN CITIES

35

52

N

1 WANNAMINGO

BERNE

57

3 MANTORVILLE

WASIOJA

2 KASSON

DODGE CENTER

6 WASECA

7 OWATONNA

14

13

NEW RICHLAND

56

90

HELMER MYRE

4 AUSTIN

5 ALBERT LEA

HUBBELL HOUSE
1854

BERNE

THE GRAND OLD MANSION

APPROX. TOTAL TOUR MILES 

INTEREST POINT 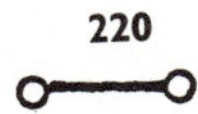

FOOD 

HISTORIC SITE 

ANTIQUES 

PARK 

SCENIC ROUTE ----

MUSEUM 

TOUR 33 PIPESTONE AND PEACE PIPES

INDIAN HISTORY

WINNEWISSA FALLS AT PIPESTONE NATIONAL MONUMENT

It would be wise to start early as this is the longest tour. What an educational trip it can be with something for everyone.

In addition to the Pipestone National Monument, the tour visits Fort Ridgely and the ancient site of the Jeffers Petroglyphs. You will see much of the history of the plains. If you can go in late July or early August, you can enjoy the "Song of Hiawatha" pageant, a remarkable presentation that is world-famous. Write or call the Hiawatha Club, Pipestone, MN 56164, 507/825-4126.

At Walnut Grove is the Laura Ingalls Wilder Museum. Here are artifacts typical of the period about which her books are written. Guided tours of the entire Pipestone downtown, including the Calumet Hotel, are given by the staff of the Pipestone County Museum, 113 S. Hiawatha, Box 175, Pipestone, MN, 507/825-5658.

INTEREST POINTS

1. FAIRFAX to REDWOOD FALLS scenic route. REDWOOD FALLS Redwood County Museum shows early transportation vehicles, 507/637-3640. Also visit the Lower Sioux Agency and the Birch Coulee Memorial.
2. WALNUT GROVE Laura Ingalls Wilder Museum, free, 507/859-2155. The pageant "Fragments of a Dream" is performed in July.
3. PIPESTONE This fascinating area has Pipestone National Monument and Cultural Center. The red stone found only here drew Indians from great distances to seek the material used for peacepipes. Indian legends are plentiful, crafts are demonstrated, and trails lead past the quarries to Lake Hiawatha and Winnewissa Falls.

   The world-famous "Song of Hiawatha" pageant is held three weekends in late July and August, and 25,000 attend each year to enjoy this spectacle that starts at sundown.

   Also visit historic downtown Pipestone, Pipestone Historical Museum and Fort Pipestone. For further information contact the Pipestone Chamber of Commerce and Tourist Center, 117 8th Ave. S.E., Box 551, Pipestone, MN 56164, 507/825-3316.
4. SLAYTON Here the Chanarambie Valley (SW of town) extends 30 miles and is crisscrossed by wagon trails, smoke pits and graveyards. Topping Buffalo Ridge are stone formations laid by Indians in ancient times.
5. LAKE SHETEK PARK at Currie. Historic cabin and End-O-Line Railroad Park.
6. WESTBROOK Old Westbrook Church (3 ½ mi. SE of MN 30) and Dutch Charlie Creek (5 mi. NE on MN 30).
7. JEFFERS PETROGLYPHS (3 mi. N of MN 30) Stone carvings 3000 BC-1700 AD, self-guided tours, 507/877-3647.
8. FORT RIDGELY STATE PARK (7 mi. S of Fairfax on MN 4) Major battle area in the Sioux uprising, fee, 507/426-7888.

RESTAURANTS ADJACENT TO TOUR

A. Prairie House Family Restaurant, MN 19, Gaylord, 507/237-5936.
B. Lyle's Cafe, MN 19, Winthrop, 507/647-9949.
C. Gannon's, MN 23, 30, and 75, Pipestone, 507/825-3114.
D. The Calumet Hotel, Main and Hiawatha, Pipestone, 507/825-5658.

TOUR 33 PIPESTONE NATIONAL MONUMENT TOUR

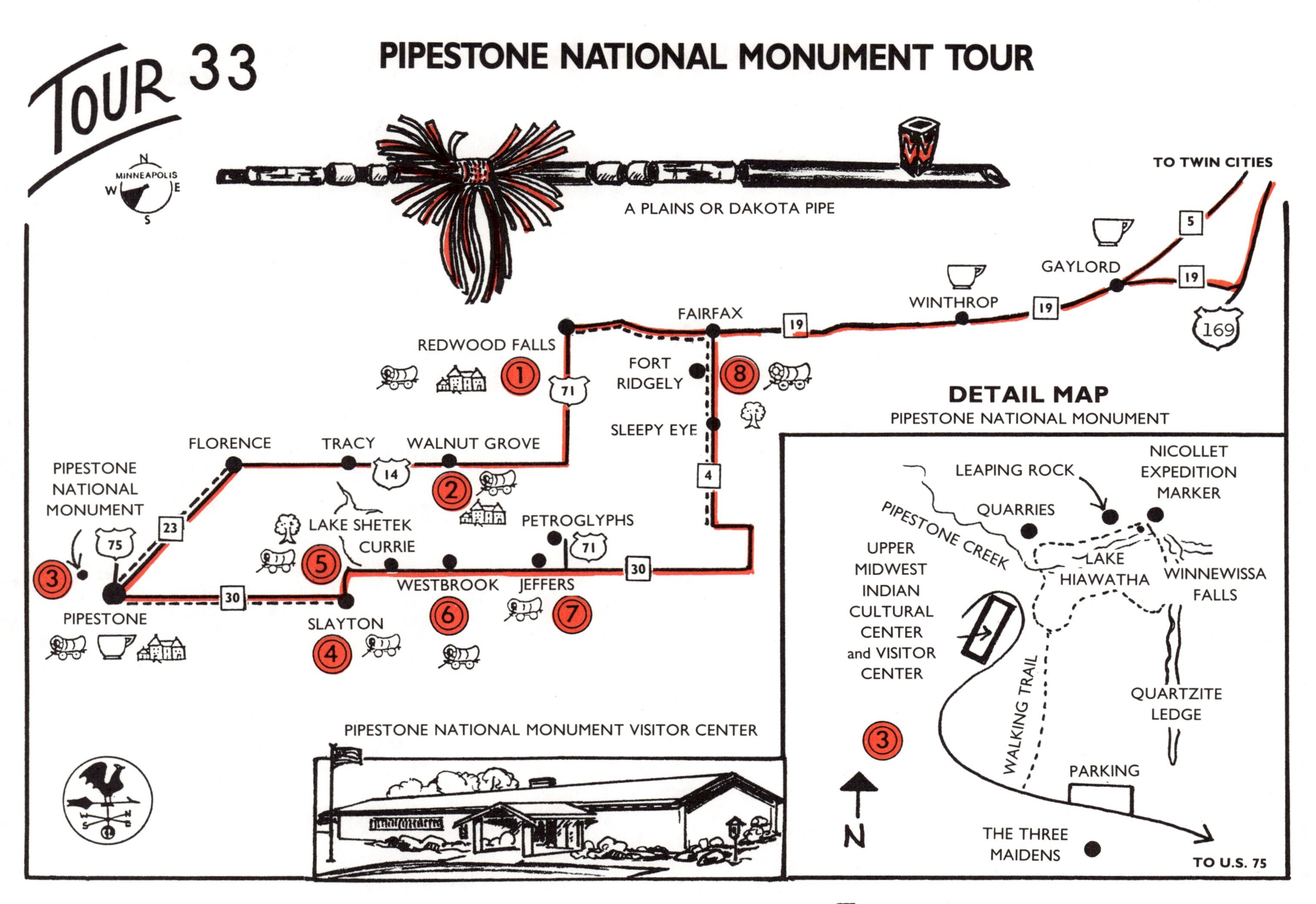

APPROX. TOTAL TOUR MILES 380

INTEREST POINT

FOOD 

HISTORIC SITE 

ANTIQUES 

PARK 

SCENIC ROUTE

MUSEUM

TOUR 34 THE BIRTHPLACE OF MINNESOTA

Stillwater, a Victorian town, is the birthplace of Minnesota. In this lovely setting you stop in time. Established on August 26, 1848, it retains nostalgia in every nook and cranny. There is something for everyone with historic inns, buildings and ornate homes. A wide choice of interest stops includes gift and speciality shops, antiques, art galleries, museums, old time foods and meats, boat, train and trolley rides, excellent dining and picnic supplies — all available in an atmosphere of friendly warmth. To really know Minnesota, stop in Stillwater for a day you will long remember; it's a visitor's favorite.

INTEREST POINTS

1. STILLWATER

   WASHINGTON COUNTY HISTORIC COURTHOUSE 1869, art gallery, Civil War memorial, first courthouse in Minnesota, exhibits, tours, S. 3rd at Pine, 612/439-6676.

   WARDEN'S HOME AND MUSEUM, 602 N. Main, open to the public.

   STAPLES MILL 1800 sawmill, N. Main St.

   HISTORICAL PLAQUE 102 S. Main St.

   OLD POST OFFICE SHOPS antiques, 220 East Myrtle, 612/439-7530.

   WINONA KNITTING MILLS 1888, 215 S. Main.

   LOWELL PARK AND LEVEE off Water St. at Myrtle.

   BRICK ALLEY Picnic supplies, books, 612/439-0266.

   STILLWATER BAKERY 612/439-9393.

   STILLWATER HONDA AND BALLOON 14399 MN 36, 612/439-1800.

   BLUFF STAIRWAY Main St. (count the steps).

   TAMARACK HOUSE GALLERIES 612/439-9393.

   SEASON'S TIQUE 209 S. Main St., 612/430-1240/633-5933.

   GRAND GARAGE AND GALLERY 324 S. Main St.

   ARCHITECTURAL WALKING TOUR Ask at shops for maps or contact the STILLWATER CHAMBER OF COMMERCE, P.O. Box 586, 101 W. Pine, Stillwater, MN, 612/439-7700.

   MINNESOTA ZEPHYR Dinner and 3-hour excursions along the St. Croix River Valley, P.O. Box 573, 601 N. Main, 55082, 612/430-3000.

   MINNESOTA TRANSPORTATION MUSEUM Myrtle and Water Sts., 612/228-0263.

   RIVERTOWN TROLLEY 715/247-3305.

   ANDIAMO RIVER BOAT 612/439-6110.

2. SOMERSET "Tubing capitol of the world" on the Apple River.

   RIVER'S EDGE, JELLYSTONE PARK AND RECREATION AREA Water slides, tubes, canoes and dining overlooking the Apple River, 2 mi. E of Somerset on WI 64, P.O. Box 67, Somerset, WI, 54025, 715/247-3305.

   BASS LAKE CHEESE FACTORY Open all year, Valley View Trail, Somerset, WI, 54025, 715/549-6617.

3. WILLOW RIVER STATE PARK Water-related activities, trails, 2,600 acres with 3 dams, 3 lakes, nature center, prairie remnants, swimming and fishing, go S from New Richmond on WI 65 to Co. Rd. A, turn W to park, 715/386-5931.

4. AAMODT'S APPLE FARM, 25 varieties of apples on 100 acres, apples and pies in a restored 1880s barn, tours, Aug.-Jan., ½ mi. N of MN 36, on Co. Rd. 15, 612/439-3127.

RESTAURANTS ADJACENT TO ROUTE

STILLWATER

A. The Freight House 1883, 305 S. Water St., 612/439-5718.

B. Lowell Inn 1927, 102 N. 2nd St., 612/439-1100.

C. Brine's 1867, lunch room and picnic supplies, 219 S. Main St., 612/439-7556.

SOMERSET

D. River's Edge, 2 mi. E of Somerset on WI 64, 715/247-3305.

TOUR 34 STILLWATER, SOMERSET and WILLOW RIVER STATE PARK

TUBING ON THE APPLE RIVER

HOT AIR BALLOON FLIGHTS

CHEESE SHOPS

N
MINNEAPOLIS
ST PAUL
W E
S

ST. CROIX RIVER

SOMERSET

NEW RICHMOND

STILLWATER

HOULTON

BAYPORT

BURKHARDT

TO ST. PAUL 20 MILES

WILLOW RIVER STATE PARK

MINNESOTA

WISCONSIN

1 2 3 4

36 64 35 64 65 95 94

V A

RIVERBOAT CRUISES

JELLYSTONE PARK

APPLE ORCHARDS

TROLLEY RIDES

TRAIN RIDES

APPROX. TOTAL TOUR MILES

INTEREST POINT

FOOD

HISTORIC SITE

ANTIQUES

PARK

SCENIC ROUTE

MUSEUM

TOUR 35

CHILDREN ON TOURS

Where can children be taken on a tour? The Twin Cities area has a wide range of educational and fun interest points. A tour for a child should be both a learning experience and a relaxation medium. Rather than visiting just one place, why not combine both goals for a dual benefit? As an example, if the first stop is serious and disciplined, why not move on to a purely light-hearted venture such as the two illustrated at the right. There are many possible combinations. Choose ones appropriate for the children's age levels.

The routes at the right demonstrate how two tours may be found in even a limited area. Each one makes a full day's outing that is rich with learning and delightful pleasure. Choose your own sites and begin to know your vicinity's historic and recreational possibilities.

Preparation and planning are necessary as successful tours don't just happen. Discuss the trip in advance. What will we see? What will be the rules of the day? Can we make name tags and arrange a buddy system? Can we draw simple maps of the route? What will we need to take — snacks, pocket change, a First Aid Kit, a picnic lunch, sing-a-long sheets and a tape recorder to preserve the sounds of the day? Will we need sweaters or jackets? Check to be sure the interest point has the hours and day reserved, if necessary, and that you are expected.

The majority of tours listed in this book are suitable for longer trips with children, either as a group or as a family. When traveling any distance, be sure to take supplies for amusement between stops. A box of crayons, paper, blunt scissors, puzzles and favorite toys can help the time pass. Can they draw something that they have seen? Can we share jokes from a book? Keep the day filled with laughter and joy for pleasant memories.

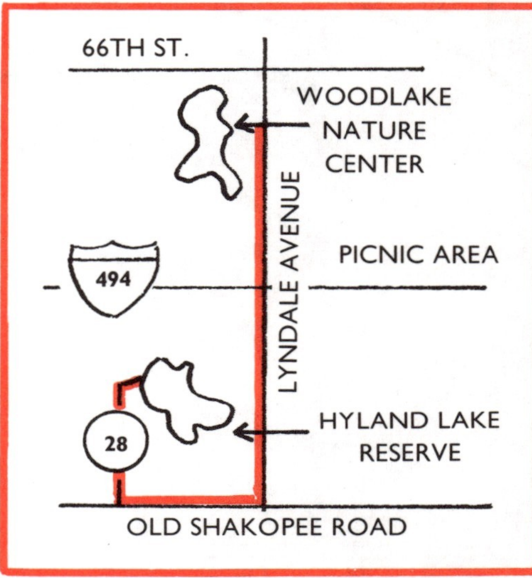

TWO LAKES TOUR

FLOWERS AND GREENERY

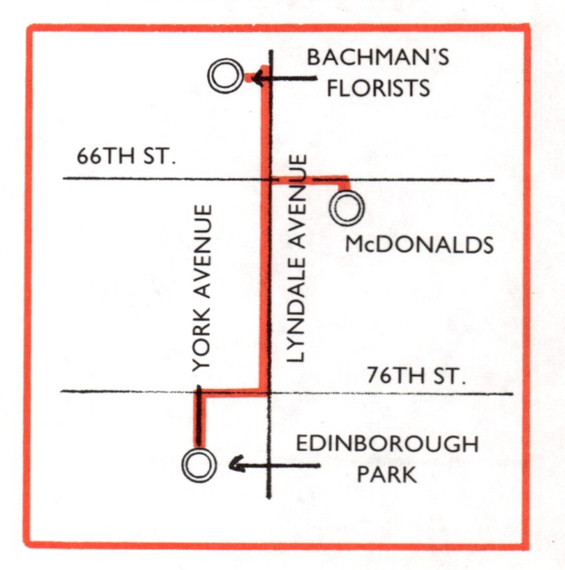

TOUR 36 DISCOVER AND EXPLORE LOCAL ATTRACTIONS

PLACES THAT EDUCATE AND ENTERTAIN

ALEXANDER RAMSEY HOUSE Historic home of Minnesota's first territorial governor, free to children, reservations, 265 S. Exchange St. at Walnut, St. Paul, 612/222-5717. See Tour 5.

AMERICAN SWEDISH INSTITUTE 33-room mansion, fee, 2600 Park Ave., Minneapolis, 612/871-4907. See Tour 15.

AMTRAK Train rides, call for schedules, Amtrak Station, 730 Transfer Rd., St. Paul, 612/644-1127.

ANIMAL HUMANE SOCIETY Film and tour, free, reservations, 845 N. Meadow Lane, Golden Valley, 612/522-4325.

ANSON NORTHRUP and BOOM ISLAND PARK Boarding dock for riverboat cruise, fee, 8th Ave. N and Plymouth Ave. Bridge, Minneapolis, 612/348-2226. See Tour 2.

BACHMAN'S FLORISTS Greenhouse tour, free, reservations, 6010 Lyndale Ave. S., Minneapolis, 612/861-7691. See Tour 15.

BANDANA SQUARE Restored railroad terminal, Children's Museum, railroad exhibit, free, 1021 Bandana Blvd. E., St. Paul, 612/647-9628. See Tour 5.

BELL MUSEUM OF NATURAL HISTORY Touch-and-See Room, permanent exhibits, fee, University of Minnesota, 17th Ave. S.E. and University Ave., Minneapolis, 612/624-7083. See Tour 2.

BROOKLYN PARK HISTORICAL FARM Living record of Minnesota farm life, fee, 4345 101st Ave. N., Brooklyn Park, 612/424-8017.

BYERLY'S FOOD STORES Self-guided tours, free, 3777 Park Center Blvd., St. Louis Park, 612/929-2100.

CHILDREN'S THEATRE COMPANY Children's literature adaptations, 2400 3rd Ave. S., Minneapolis, 612/874-0400.

COMO PARK, ZOO, CONSERVATORY, COMO LAKE All-day fun, N. Lexington Pkwy. and Como Ave., St. Paul, zoo free, conservatory small fee, 612/489-1740. See Tour 5.

EDINBOROUGH PARK See Tour 30.

ELOISE BUTLER WILDFLOWER GARDEN AND BIRD SANCTUARY. See Tour 18.

FEDERAL RESERVE BANK OF MINNEAPOLIS Currency story, free, 612/340-2446. See Tour 9.

FIRE FIGHTERS MEMORIAL MUSEUM See Tour 10.

FORT SNELLING STATE PARK Living history of military base, museum, fee, Post Rd. off MN 5, St. Paul. 612/727-1961. See Tour 27.

GIBBS FARM MUSEUM See Tour 5.

HYLAND LAKE PARK RESERVE AND RECREATION CENTER Chutes and ladders, picnic sites, trails, free. 10145 E. Bush Lake Rd., Bloomington, 612/941-4362. See Tour 25.

HENNEPIN COUNTY HISTORICAL SOCIETY MUSEUM Free, 2303 3rd Ave. S., Minneapolis, 612/870-1329. See Tour 15.

LAKE HARRIET PARK Bandshell, rose garden, bird sanctuary, rock garden, free; streetcar, fee; *Queen of the Lakes* boat ride, fee; E. Lake Harriet Pkwy., Minneapolis, 612/348-2226. See Tour 18.

MINNEAPOLIS FIRE DEPARTMENT STATION Unusual design, 121 E. 15th St., 612/348-7528. See Tour 10.

MINNEAPOLIS PUBLIC LIBRARY PLANETORIUM Free, 300 Nicollet Mall, 612/372-6644. See Tour 9.

MINNEHAHA FALLS AND PARK See Tour 27.

MINNESOTA AIR GUARD MUSEUM See Tour 10.

MINNESOTA VALLEY NATIONAL WILDLIFE REFUGE See Tour 25.

MINNESOTA ZOOLOGICAL GARDEN See Tour 12.

MURPHY'S LANDING See Tour 21.

PADELFORD PACKET BOAT CO., *Jonathon Padelford* and *Josiah Snelling*, fee, Harriet Island, St. Paul, 612/227-1100.

RICHFIELD WOODLAKE NATURE CENTER See Tour 25.

SCIENCE MUSEUM OF MINNESOTA See Tour 4.

TOWN SQUARE PARK Enclosed park with waterfalls, greenery, free, 7th and Minnesota Sts., St. Paul, 612/291-8900. See Tour 4.

UNIVERSITY OF MINNESOTA LANDSCAPE ARBORETUM See Tour 1.

VALLEYFAIR FAMILY AMUSEMENT PARK See Tour 21.

ARE YOU A VISITOR?

HERE ARE HELPFUL IDEAS TO MAKE EXPLORING MINNESOTA EASY

What else is there to SEE and DO in the Twin Cities and Minnesota?

For tourist information stop at the EXPLORE MINNESOTA, Mall of America, USA, N129 North Garden, Bloomington, Minnesota. 612/853-0182.

MORE IDEAS: Check the local yellow pages of the telephone directory. Here are listings of entertainment, historic, sight-seeing and transportation to round out your visit to the Mall of America.

- Car Rental
- Airlines
- Hotels/Motels
- Sight-seeing buses,
- Trains/Amtrak 612/644-1127
- Theatres
- Art Studios/Galleries
- Zoos/Refuges
- Restaurants/Resorts
- Sports
- Area history
- Parks/Recreation
- Museums/Gift Shops
- Events calendar
- Golf Courses
- Churches
- Entertainment

•See page 75 (this book) for ideas to extend your visit.

EXPLORE AND VENTURE OUT —
MINNESOTA IS EXCITING AND BEAUTIFUL

THE EXPLORE MINNESOTA SHOP

AT THE MALL OF AMERICA

Here's the place to discover other interesting travel information, gift items as well as the opportunity to plan and book an area get-a-way. Co-operating are the Minnesota Office of Tourism, the Minnesota Department of Natural Resources, the Minnesota Historical Society and the Minnesota State Arts Board.

State park permits and hunting and fishing licences will be sold as well. Computerized information, brochures and personal trip planning assistance in addition to lodging reservations — all these assets will help round out further exploration of Minnesota. The EXPLORE MINNESOTA SHOP is there to help you. Located at N129 North Garden, Mall of Minnesota. 612/853-0182.

THE LOG CHUTE
CAMP SNOOPY
There's a place for fun in your life

EXPERIENCE THE

MALL OF AMERICA

The MALL OF AMERICA is the largest fully enclosed retail and family entertainment complex in the United States. Over 400 specialty stores, Knott's Camp Snoopy and several other attractions join anchor stores Bloomingdales, Macy's, Nordstrom and Sears.

The location in Bloomington is just five minutes from the Minneapolis-St. Paul International Airport and just 10 miles from downtown Minneapolis and St. Paul. In this 73 acre mall will be found shops, attractions, shows, food, and an amazing Underwater World. The visitors, with instructional headphones, are surrounded by aquatic life.

KNOTT'S CAMP SNOOPY

Knott's Camp Snoopy offers a multitude of excitement in the largest indoor themed entertainment park in America. There's twenty-one rides and attractions, shops, four entertainment stages . . . eight places to eat. It all adds up to a world of fun for the whole family.

Welcome to endless adventure!
5000 Center Court 612/883-8600

UNDERWATER WORLD
The same planet but a different world — Mall of America

TWO HISTORIC AND SCENIC TROLLEY RIDES

MINNEAPOLIS
RIVERCITY TROLLEY

Would you like to see Minneapolis on a historically narrated trolley? Tours last approximately sixty-five minutes. There are starting points at the Minneapolis Convention Center, Walker Art Center and St. Anthony Main. The trolleys run every twenty minutes and travel through the Warehouse district, Sculpture Garden, the Stone Arch Bridge and many other interesting places. Hours are M-F 10-4, Sat. 10-4 and Sun 10-5. 612/204-0000.

ST. PAUL
CAPITOL CITY TROLLEY

Here's a fun and informative way to get to know St. Paul. You will learn the history as you drive by the State Capitol, City Center, Kellogg Boulevard, view the Mississippi River and interesting areas. Starting points are Park Square, the Capitol and the World Trade Center. Hours are M-F 8-5, Sat. 11-4 and Sun. 11-5. 612/223-5600

DO YOU KNOW

MINNESOTA means "Sky-tinted Waters".

STATE SYMBOLS

SEAL The State Seal depicts a homesteader. The motto is *L'Etoile du Nord*, "Star of the North."

BIRD The Common Loon is the State Bird. Its lonely cry is haunting on northern lakes.

FLOWER The Showy Pink Lady's Slipper is the lovely State Flower.

TREE The Red or Norway Pine is the State Tree, a stately symbol.

FISH The Walleye is Minnesota's State Fish.

GEMSTONE The Lake Superior Agate is the State Gem Stone.

CAPITAL St. Paul is Minnesota's State Capital.

LARGEST CITY Minneapolis, the "City of Lakes," is the largest city in Minnesota.

NORTHERNMOST POINT OF LOWER 48 STATES The Northwest Angle has this distinction. Minnesota is 348 miles wide and 406 miles long.

INTERESTING PLACES

MINNEHAHA FALLS is the highest falls in a metropolitan area in the United States.

PAUL BUNYAN and his blue ox Babe are Minnesota legendary figures at Bemidji.

FORT SNELLING has the oldest existing buildings in Minnesota.

SPLIT ROCK LIGHTHOUSE on Lake Superior's North Shore is a well-known landmark.

ITASCA STATE PARK is where the mighty Mississippi originates.

WATERSKIING was originated at Lake Pepin near Lake City.

MAYOWOOD at Rochester was the home of Charles Mayo, medical pioneer.

PIPESTONE NATIONAL MONUMENT encompasses quarries of pipestone used in Indian pipes and artifacts.

LITTLE FALLS is the site of Charles Lindbergh's boyhood home.

RESOURCES TO HELP YOU TRAVEL

Short on time? Choose part of a tour or follow the entire route to get an overview and return later to places that had special appeal to you.

Long on time? Combine two or more adjacent tours and plan to camp or stay overnight at one of Minnesota's fine motels or Bed and Breakfast homes.

Casual or deluxe? It's up to you, as either way you will enjoy your day. Whether you picnic or eat out you will find accommodations abundant in Minnesota.

You can enlarge your knowledge of Minnesota's natural beauty and assets if you take advantage of the many invaluable resource materials available from state departments. Listed are some of the departments and the pamphlets, brochures and maps that you may request. Call or write for these tour aids and carry them with you.

Inclusion in this guide does not constitute endorsement. It is intended as a general tour aid and there may be omissions or errors.

MINNEAPOLIS CHAMBER OF COMMERCE
81 S. 9th St. 370-9132
ST. PAUL AREA CHAMBER OF COMMERCE
445 Minnesota St. 223-5000.
HIGHWAY EMERGENCY NUMBER
DIAL 0, Call Zenith 7000
MINNESOTA STATE PATROL
WEATHER 612/375-0830

"WISE UP" YOUR FAMILY, VISITORS OR GROUP TO THE ATTRACTIONS OF THE TWIN CITY AREA

HAIL! MINNESOTA

Minnesota Hail to thee!
Hail to thee our state so dear,
Thy light shall ever be
A beacon bright and clear.
Thy sons and daughters true
Will proclaim thee near and far,
They will guard thy fame and
adore thy name;
Thou shalt be their Northern Star.

RESOURCE SUGGESTIONS

Minnesota Tourist Information Center, 430 Cedar St. S., St. Paul, MN 55101, 612/296-5029, tollfree in MN 1-800/652-9747. Out-of-state call 1-800-657-3700.

EXPLORE MINNESOTA, MALL OF AMERICA, N129 North Garden, Bloomington, MN 55425, 612/853-0182

Minnesota Department of Natural Resources, Centennial Office Bldg., 658 Cedar St., St. Paul, MN 55155, 612/296-6157.

Minneapolis Parks and Recreation, 310 4th Ave. S., Mpls., MN 55415, 612-348-2243.

Ramsey County Parks and Recreation, 1850 White Bear Ave. N., St. Paul, MN 55109, 612/777-1361.

Hennepin County Park Reserve District, Box 296, Maple Plain, MN 55359, 612/473-4693.

St. Paul Parks and Forestry, 1224 N. Lexington Pkwy., St. Paul, MN 55103, 612/488-7291.

Anoka County Parks Department, 550 Bunker Lake Blvd., Anoka, MN 55303, 612/757-3920.

Minnesota Historical Society Historic Sites, Fort Snelling Branch, Bldg. 25, Fort Snelling, MN 55111, 612/726-1171.

American Camping Association, 4132 88th Lane N.W., Blaine, MN 55433, 612/784-5400.

For a catalog listing publications such as lake maps and county maps, write: Minnesota State Publications, Documents Section, Room 140, Centennial Bldg., St. Paul, MN 55155.

HAPPY MEMORIES

Precious memories are the best souvenirs that you can take home from any trip. To achieve this, here are basic tour suggestions that will assure a pleasant travel experience.

PLAN AHEAD

The success of your tour depends on this important preparation. A brief time spent making phone calls or contacting a local information source will smooth the way. Advance planning and reservations help avoid disappointment. Telephone numbers and Chamber of Commerce or Tourist Information organizations are listed to assist in plans. Due to frequent changes in the hours or days places are open to the public, it is difficult to keep information accurate or current. An advance call from the interest point where you are located to the next destination will often answer your question.

TOUR MAPS

Maps are intended to stimulate enthusiasm and have been kept simple to emphasize the colored tour outline. Be sure to carry official state highway maps, campground guides, if needed, boat launch sites and fishing or winter recreation information. Note the resource listings on page 79. Approximate mileage is given for each tour, but the state map will provide distances from point to point. Side trips and route diversions may alter mileage projections.

DISCOVERIES ALONG THE WAY

Stop to read the historical markers as they provide valuable background data for particular areas. Restaurants and shops can not all be listed and those included are primarily adjacent to the tour route. You will discover others along the way.

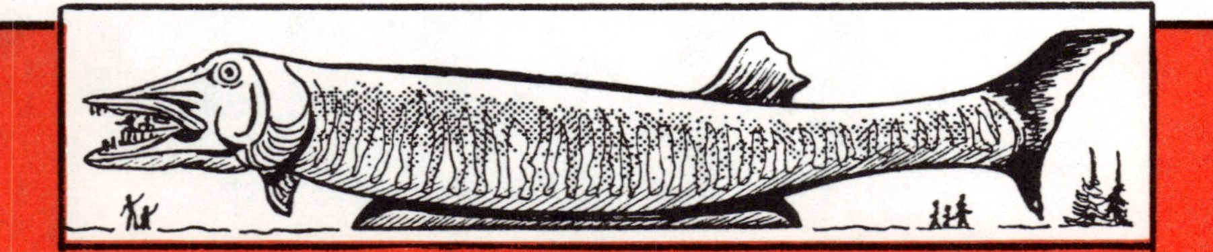